BENCHMARK SERIES

Microsoft® Word 2016 Desktop Publishing

Workbook

Roggenkamp • Rutkosky • Arford

St. Paul

Senior Vice President	Linda Hein
Editor in Chief	Christine Hurney
Managing Editor	Cheryl Drivdahl
Assistant Developmental Editor	Katie Werdick
Testers and Instructional Support Writers	Janet Blum, Fanshawe College; Traci J. H. Post; Brienna McWade
Director of Production	Timothy W. Larson
Production Editor	Jen Weaverling
Cover and Text Designer	Valerie King
Senior Design and Production Specialist	Jack Ross
Copy Editor	Communicáto, Ltd.
Proofreader	Shannon Kottke
Indexer	Terry Casey
Vice President Information Technology	Chuck Bratton
Digital Projects Manager	Tom Modl
Vice President Sales and Marketing	Scott Burns
Director of Marketing	Lara Weber McLellan

Cover Photo Credits: © Photomall/Dreamstime.

ISBN 978-0-76387-616-6 (print)

875 Montreal Way
St. Paul, MN 55102
Email: educate@emcp.com
Website: ParadigmEducation.com

Printed in the United States of America

25 24 23 22 21 20 19 18 17   3 4 5 6 7 8 9 10

Contents

Microsoft®

Word Desktop Publishing

Unit 1

Understanding and Applying Desktop Publishing Concepts

Understanding Desktop Publishing

CHAPTER 1

Study Tools

Study tools include a presentation and a glossary. Use these resources to help you further develop and review skills learned in this chapter.

Concepts Check

Check your understanding by identifying application tools used in this chapter. If you are a SNAP user, launch the Concepts Check from your Assignments page.

Recheck

Check your understanding by taking this quiz. If you are a SNAP user, launch the Recheck from your Assignments page.

Skills Assessment

Assessment 1

Data Files

Evaluate Documents

Many well-designed and many poorly designed documents can be found on the Internet. Looking critically at as many publications as possible will give you a sense of what works and what does not. In this skill assessment, find two different examples of documents—flyers, newsletters, resumes, brochures, business cards, announcements, certificates, and so on—and print hard copies of both. Evaluate these documents according to the desktop publishing concepts discussed in this chapter using **DocumentAnalysisGuide.docx**. To do this, complete the following steps:

1. Open **DocumentAnalysisGuide.docx** and then save it with the name **1-Analysis-1A**.
2. Complete the Document Analysis Guide for the first example document (type Assessment 1A on the *Exercise #* line) and then save and print **1-Analysis-1A.docx**. Attach the printed evaluation guide to the front of the printed example document. Close **1-Analysis-1A.docx**.
3. Open **DocumentAnalysisGuide.docx** and then save it with the name **1-Analysis-1B**.
4. Complete the Document Analysis Guide for the second example document (type Assessment 1B on the *Exercise #* line) and then save and print **1-Analysis-1B.docx**. Attach the printed evaluation guide to the front of the other printed example document. Close **1-Analysis-1B.docx**.

Assessment 2

Arrange Design Elements in a Flyer

1. Open **HappySummerFlyer.docx** and then save it with the name **1-HappySummer**.
2. Apply the design principles discussed in Chapter 1 to create a professional-looking advertisement for the Happy Summer Nursery. Eight design elements have been created and placed randomly on the page. Rearrange the text boxes and graphics to create a harmonious design that attracts attention and reinforces the message. Make the following changes:
   a. Click and drag each design element to create a layout with good directional flow.
   b. Apply a different theme.
   c. Make sure all the fonts are consistently used and that the text is appropriately sized.
3. Save, print, and then close **1-HappySummer.docx**.

Assessment

Use the Internet to Research Elements of Professional Design

1. Access your favorite search engine and then search for at least 10 elements that comprise a professional-looking flyer, brochure, or newsletter.
2. Working with a group of two or three students, combine your notes into a fact sheet, using a table to help organize your findings.
3. Use any Word 2016 features that you are familiar with to enhance the design and layout of your fact sheet. Refer to Figure WB-1.1 as a guide to the type of information to include in your document.
4. Below the table, provide your sources. If necessary, review a current reference manual or search the Internet to find the appropriate format for typing your sources.
5. Save the completed fact sheet and name it **1-ElementsFacts**.
6. Print a copy for each member of your class and then close the document.

Assessment

Draw a Thumbnail Sketch to Plan a Document

Working with two or three other students, create a flyer for one of the situations described below. Start by drawing a thumbnail sketch using lines, boxes, and rough illustrations to plan the placement of text and graphics on the page. As a group, discuss how to include focus, balance, proportion, contrast, white space, directional flow, and consistency in your flyer. Be sure to consider the purpose and target audience for the situation. Designate areas in your sketch for such items as time, date, location, and response information. Label your sketch **1-Sketch**. Next, create the final flyer in Word and name it **1-Flyer**. Elect one person on your team to act as a spokesperson for your group to explain how your team used the design elements discussed in Chapter 1 in creating your flyer.

Situation 1: Volunteer project

Situation 2: Software-training seminar

Figure WB-1.1 Sample Solution for Assessment 3

By: Student Name Here

Nameplate	The nameplate is the banner on the front of a newsletter that identifies the publication and may also contain graphics, logos, a subtitle, a motto, and publication information such as the volume, issue, or date.
Body	The body contains the majority of the text excluding the headlines and decorative elements.
Table of Contents	The table of contents is a brief list of the articles and sections in the newsletter, along with page numbers for corresponding items, and usually displays on the front page.
Masthead	The masthead lists the publisher and other pertinent data, such as staff names, subscription information, and addresses.
Headings and Titles	Headings and titles create a hierarchy that helps lead the reader through the newsletter.
Page Numbers	Page numbers may appear at the top, bottom, or sides of the newsletter pages.
Byline	The byline usually displays between the headline and the beginning of the text, and includes a short paragraph that provides the name of the article author.
Continuation Line	A continuation line is used to help readers find the remainder of an article that spans two or more pages.
End Sign	An end sign is a symbol that indicates to the reader the end of an article.
Pull Quote	A pull quote is a small selection of text that is pulled out to attract the reader's attention and usually displays in a larger typeface.
Photos and Illustrations	Photos and illustrations are used to enhance the visual appearance of the newsletter.
Mailing Panel	The mailing panel is the section of the newsletter that contains the return address, mailing address, and postage.

Source: Howard Bear, Jacci. "12 Parts of a Newsletter." *About.com.* Web. 14 August 2013.

Assessment 5

Data Files

Evaluate a Promotional Document

Evaluate a poorly designed flyer according to the items listed on the **DocumentAnalysisGuide.docx** document.

1. Open **DocumentAnalysisGuide.docx** and then save it with the name **1-Analysis-5**.
2. Open **CleaningFlyer.docx**.
3. Print one copy and then close **CleaningFlyer.docx**.
4. Complete the Document Analysis Guide. At the end of the document, list three suggestions for improvements.

Visual Benchmark

Create a Flyer from a Template

1. At a blank document, display the New backstage area and search the online templates for a flyer by typing spring flyer in the search text box and then pressing the Enter key. Double-click the template similar to what is shown in Figure WB-1.2 on page WB-8. ***Note: If this template is not available, use SpringFlyer.docx located in the C1 folder.***
2. At the new document, enter the information shown in Figure WB-1.2.
3. Add any graphics that may enhance the document, such as the bird added to Figure WB-1.2.
4. Save the completed flyer and name it **1-SpringFlyer**.
5. Print and then close the document.

Case Study

Part 1

Data Files

You are the assistant to Paul Brewster, the marketing coordinator at a medium-sized flight school. You have been asked by Mr. Brewster to prepare a flyer for a special being offered for the first hour of flight. Mr. Brewster has already created the Word document **FlightFlyer.docx**, which includes all the necessary information and company graphics. Open **FlightFlyer.docx** and save it with the name **1-FlightFlyer-CS1**. Rearrange the elements in the document and then use any Word 2016 elements you have learned in Chapter 1 to enhance the design of the flyer. Save, print, and then close **1-FlightFlyer-CS1.docx**.

Part 2

Data Files

When designing a document, it can be useful to develop two or more different versions. With multiple versions to consider, the document that communicates the message in the best way and is more appealing can be chosen for publication. Furthermore, the chosen document can be modified using some of the elements from the other version. Mr. Brewster would like you to create a second version of the **FlightFlyer.docx** document. Open **FlightFlyer.docx** and save it with the name **1-FlightFlyer-CS2**. Rearrange the elements in the document in a different way than you did in Part 1. (Consider changing the page orientation, symmetry, and contrast.) Also use any Word 2016 elements you have learned in Chapter 1 to enhance the design of the flyer. Save, print, and then close **1-FlightFlyer-CS2.docx**.

Part

3

Data Files

Now that you have completed two flyers, compare them and choose the one that best communicates the message clearly and is most visually appealing. Pick some elements from the other flyer that will work well in the flyer you have chosen and then add them to the final flyer. Save the final flyer and name it **1-FlightFlyer-CS3**. Print and then close the document. Evaluate your final flyer by completing the following steps:

1. Open **DocumentAnalysisGuide.docx** and then save it with the name **1-Analysis-CS3**.
2. Complete the Document Analysis Guide for the final flyer and then save and print **1-Analysis-CS3.docx**.
3. Staple together hard copies of **1-FlightFlyer-CS3.docx** and **1-Analysis-CS3.docx** and then turn them in to your instructor.

Part

4

Data Files

A great way to learn different design elements that can be used in a new document is to evaluate a similar document. Exchange copies of your final flyer with another classmate either as hard copy or through email. Review and evaluate your classmate's document by completing the following steps:

1. Open **DocumentAnalysisGuide.docx** and then save it with the name **1-Analysis-CS4**.
2. Complete the Document Analysis Guide for your classmate's final flyer and then save and print **1-Analysis-CS4.docx**.

Figure WB-1.2 Visual Benchmark

You're invited to the 14th annual

spring fling
celebration

Come to the Spring Fling celebration and be prepared for a day of games, dancing, sweets, and family!

Where: **Stamford Suites**

When: **April 21, 2018**

Time: **Noon to 3:00 p.m.**

CHAPTER 2

Applying and Modifying Fonts

Study Tools

Study tools include a presentation and a glossary. Use these resources to help you further develop and review skills learned in this chapter.

Concepts Check

Check your understanding by identifying application tools used in this chapter. If you are a SNAP user, launch the Concepts Check from your Assignments page.

Recheck

Check your understanding by taking this quiz. If you are a SNAP user, launch the Recheck from your Assignments page.

Skills Assessment

Assessment 1

Data Files

Format a Training Flyer

1. Open **CWFlyer.docx** and then save it with the name **2-CWFlyer**.
2. Select the text in the text box at the top of the flyer, change the font to 26-point Cambria, apply bold formatting and the small caps effect, and then change the RGB colors to Red: 60, Green: 130, and Blue: 200. ***Hint: Change the RGB colors with options in the Colors dialog box with the Custom tab selected.***
3. Select the text *Workplace Shortcuts for Preparing Office Documents* and then change the font to 36-point Cambria and apply the small caps effect.
4. Select the text beginning with *Jules Mason* and ending with *Room 205* and then change the font to 12-point Cambria and apply italic formatting.
5. Select the date in the lower right corner of the document, change the font to 14-point Cambria, apply bold and italic formatting, and then apply the same RGB colors that were applied to the text in the text box (Red: 60, Green: 130, and Blue: 200). Your document should appear similar to the document shown in Figure WB-2.1.
6. Save, print, and then close **2-CWFlyer.docx**.

Figure WB-2.1 Flyer Formatted in Assessment 1

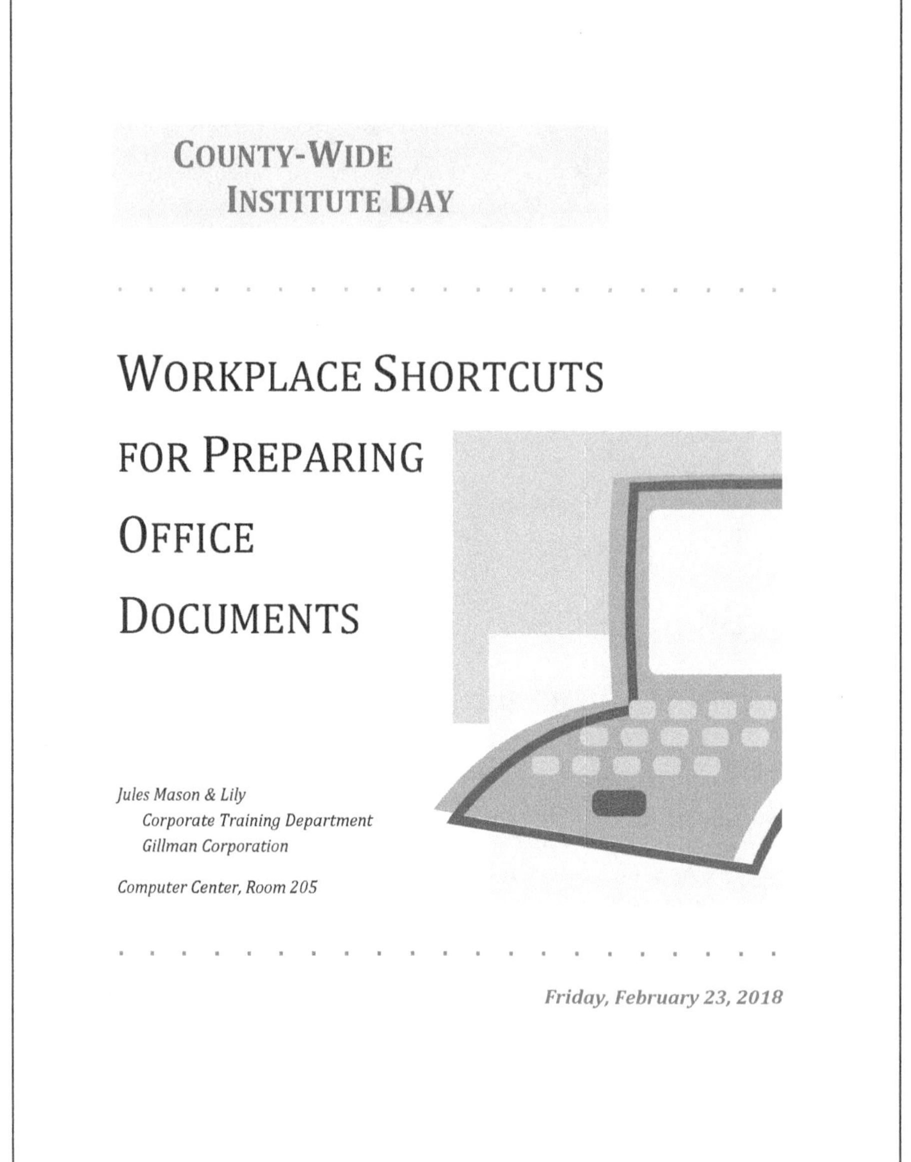

Assessment 2 Format a Meeting Agenda

Data Files

1. Open **DominicanAgenda.docx** and then save it with the name **2-DominicanAgenda**.
2. Apply the Quotable theme and the Blue Green theme colors.
3. Type text in the document as shown in Figure WB-2.2 with the following specifications:
   a. Type the first three lines of text. (Press the Down Arrow key, rather than the Enter key, to move to the next line.) Make sure the text is set in 26-point Century Gothic and then apply the Blue, Accent 6, Darker 25% font color.
   b. Type the text Delegates' Program in the fourth line of the document, set it in 20-point Century Gothic, and then apply bold and italic formatting and the Fill: Aqua, Accent color 2; Outline: Aqua, Accent color 2 text effect (third column, first row).

c. Type the times in the first column of the table, as shown in Figure WB-2.2. Insert an en dash between the times in each time period (e.g., 12:30–16:00).
d. Insert the registered symbol (®) immediately to the right of the company name, *Leading Edge Consultants*, which appears about halfway down the second column of the table. Make sure the symbol displays as a superscript character.
e. Select the space between the words *address* and *Ambassador* (in the second column in the second row from the bottom of the page) and then insert an em dash.

4. Make sure the content fits on one page. If necessary, delete blank lines or decrease the spacing before or after paragraphs to ensure the text fits on one page.
5. Save, print, and then close **2-DominicanAgenda.docx**.

Figure WB-2.2 Meeting Agenda Formatted in Assessment 2

2018 Annual Meeting
Casa de Campo
Dominican Republic

Delegates' Program

Saturday, November 3	
12:30–16:00	Business meetings (starting with lunch)
17:00–18:15	First-time attendees' meeting and reception
18:30	Transportation of participants to Las Minitas Beach
Sunday, November 4	
07:00–08:15	Breakfast
08:30–09:00	Opening ceremony
09:15–10:45	***"A Time for Change"*** presentation by Dr. Carl Wilhelm, President, Leading Edge Consultants®
10:45–11:15	Break
11:15–12:15	***"An International Perspective"*** presentation by Samuel Reed, President and CEO, Global Management, LLP
12:30–13:30	Summary of report on regional specialties Lunch
13:45–15:30	Breakout sessions on specialties Remainder of afternoon free for networking
Evening	Regional dinners
Monday, November 5	
09:00–10:00	***"Business Opportunities in Emerging Markets"*** presentation by Julia Reyes, President, Reyes Associates
10:00–10:30	Break
10:30–11:30	Keynote address—Ambassador Author Smith
11:30	Adjournment

Assessment 3

Data Files

Research and Develop a Workstation Ergonomics Fact Sheet

You work for Horizon Cardiologists. You have been asked to research information on laptop ergonomics and then include your findings in the document titled **HorizonCard.docx**. You have also been asked to apply formatting to the document to improve its appearance. Figure WB-2.3 shows a sample solution for formatting the document.

1. Open **HorizonCard.docx** then save it with the name **2-HorizonCard**.
2. Use an Internet search engine to research information on laptop ergonomics and then include that information as bulleted text below the new heading *Laptop Ergonomics*. Add the source information for the website you used below the current source in the document.
3. Apply a minimum of the following formatting to the document:
   - styles to the heading and subheadings
   - a style set
   - a theme
   - theme colors
   - Include a symbol in the clinic address and insert an em dash in place of the two hyphens in the text *"Healthy heart--healthy life"* at the bottom of the document.
   - Apply any additional formatting to improve the appearance of the document, and make sure all the text fits on one page.
4. Save, print, and then close **2-HorizonCard.docx**.

Figure WB-2.3 Sample Solution for Assessment 3

Horizon Cardiologists

4525 Horizon Boulevard ♥ Tampa, FL 33603 ♥ 305.555.0995

Computer Workstations

The term *ergonomics* refers to the study of workplace design and how equipment used in the office can be best designed for comfort and efficiency. This workstation fact sheet provides suggestions on how to arrange yourself at your workstation to minimize strain and maximize comfort. According to information at the Occupational Safety & Health Administration United States Department of Labor website, there are basic design goals to consider when arranging a workstation and performing computer-related tasks.

Workstation Environment

- Minimize glare from overhead lights and windows.
- Maintain air circulation.
- Do not sit directly below an air conditioning vent.

Workstation Posture

- The top of the computer monitor should be at or just below eye level.
- Your head and neck should be balanced and in line with your body.
- Keep your shoulders relaxed.
- Support your lower back using the lumbar support of your office chair.
- Keep your wrists and hands in line with your forearms.
- Keep your feet flat on the floor.

Laptop Ergonomics

- Use a chair without arms so you can move your arms.
- If possible, use a regular keyboard, mouse, and monitor.
- If you are using the laptop keyboard, do not rest your wrists while typing.
- When looking at the laptop screen, try not to bend your neck and head forward; instead tuck in your chin to look down.

Sources:

"Computer Workstations." United States Department of Labor. Web. 20 August 2017.

"Laptop Ergonomics." University of Minnesota. Web. 20 August 2017.

"Healthy heart—healthy life"

Visual Benchmark

Format a Fundraiser Invitation

Data Files

1. Open **MardiGrasInv.docx** and then save it with the name **2-MardiGrasInv**.
2. Format the document so it appears as shown in Figure WB-2.4 with the following specifications:
   a. Change the paragraph alignment for the body of the invitation, as shown in Figure WB-2.3.
   b. Set the first line of text and the last two lines of text in the document in 14-point Calibri and then apply italic formatting.
   c. Set the two lines of text *Mardi Gras Fundraiser for Summit Outreach* in 42-point Gabriola and then apply the Gradient Fill: Purple, Accent color 4; Outline: Purple, Accent color 4 text effect (third column, second row). Display the Font dialog box with the Advanced tab selected, change the *Scale* option to *90%*, turn on kerning at 14 points and above, apply stylistic set 7, and then close the dialog box.
   d. Change the font of the right-aligned text to 16-point Harrington.
   e. Replace the hyphen between *5:30* and *9:30 p.m.* with an en dash.
   f. Move and size the two horizontal lines as shown in Figure WB-2.4.
3. Save, print, and then close **2-MardiGrasInv.docx**.

Figure WB-2.4 Invitation Formatted in Visual Benchmark

Case Study

Part 1

Data Files

You work for Alpine Animal Center, and one of your job responsibilities is preparing documents for the center. The center regularly offers classes on choosing a pet, obedience training, and pet care. Open **AACTraining.docx** and then save it with the name **2-AACTraining**. Using the information you learned in this chapter, apply font and paragraph formatting to enhance the appearance of the document. When formatting the document, choose appropriate fonts, font sizes, typestyles, and font colors. Consider changing the character spacing, kerning, and word and line spacing. Insert an en dash and smart quotes where appropriate. Position the quote at the end of the document (above the footer) and then apply a stylistic set to the quote. If necessary, remove any extra spaces above and below paragraphs of text to ensure the image remains on the first page of the document. Save and then print **2-AACTraining.docx**.

Part 2

Since the Alpine Animal Center offers classes on a regular basis, you decide to create a document that provides the steps for formatting future documents for classes. With **2-AACTraining.docx** open, open a new blank document and then type information on the formatting you applied to **2-AACTraining.docx**. Include specific information such as the fonts, font sizes, typestyles, and font colors. Also include any character spacing, kerning, and word and line spacing formatting that was applied. Save the completed document and name it **2-AACFormatting**. Print and then close **2-AACFormatting.docx** and then close **2-AACTraining.docx**.

Part 3

Data Files

Open **AACPetCare.docx** and then save it with the name **2-AACPetCare**. Using the formatting document you prepared, apply similar formatting to **2-AACPetCare.docx**. If necessary, remove any extra spaces above and below paragraphs of text to ensure the image remains on the first page of the document. Save, print, and then close the document.

Part 4

Data Files

One of the veterinarians at Alpine Animal Center is interested in offering a one-hour class on tips for choosing the right pet. Open **AACChoosingPet.docx** and then save it with the name **2-AACChoosingPet**. Using the Internet, search for information on how to choose a pet. With the information you find, type text in the document such as the class name, a brief description, topics covered, and the class date and time. Consider inserting an image in the document, and apply similar formatting to the document as you did to the other two center documents (**2-AACTraining.docx** and **2-AACPetCare.docx**). Save, print, and then close **2-AACChoosingPet.docx**.

Creating Personal Documents and Templates

CHAPTER 3

Study Tools

Study tools include a presentation and a glossary. Use these resources to help you further develop and review skills learned in this chapter.

Concepts Check

Check your understanding by identifying application tools used in this chapter. If you are a SNAP user, launch the Concepts Check from your Assignments page.

Recheck

Check your understanding by taking this quiz. If you are a SNAP user, launch the Recheck from your Assignments page.

Skills Assessment

Assessment 1

Data Files

Create a Change-of-Address Postcard

Create the change-of-address postcard shown in Figure WB-3.1 with the following specifications:

1. At a blank document, display the Label Options dialog box and then choose the *Avery US Letter 8386 Postcards* option, which contains labels that measure 4 inches by 6 inches.
2. Follow the instructions in the callouts in Figure WB-3.1 to create the postcard; however, use your name and address and address the postcard as if you were sending it to a friend.
3. Insert **postage.png** located in the C3 folder. When inserting the image on the back of the card (in the bottom table cell), make sure the insertion point is positioned in the upper left corner of the bottom table cell and not inside the text box containing the blue border.
4. Use the Papyrus font or a similar font if Papyrus is not available.
5. Insert the triangle shape on the front of the postcard, which is located in the Shapes button drop-down list.
6. Apply outside borders to both the front and back of the postcard.
7. Group any related objects.
8. Save the document with the name **3-AddressChange**.
9. Print and then close **3-AddressChange.docx**.

Figure WB-3.1 Change-of-Address Postcard Created in Assessment 1

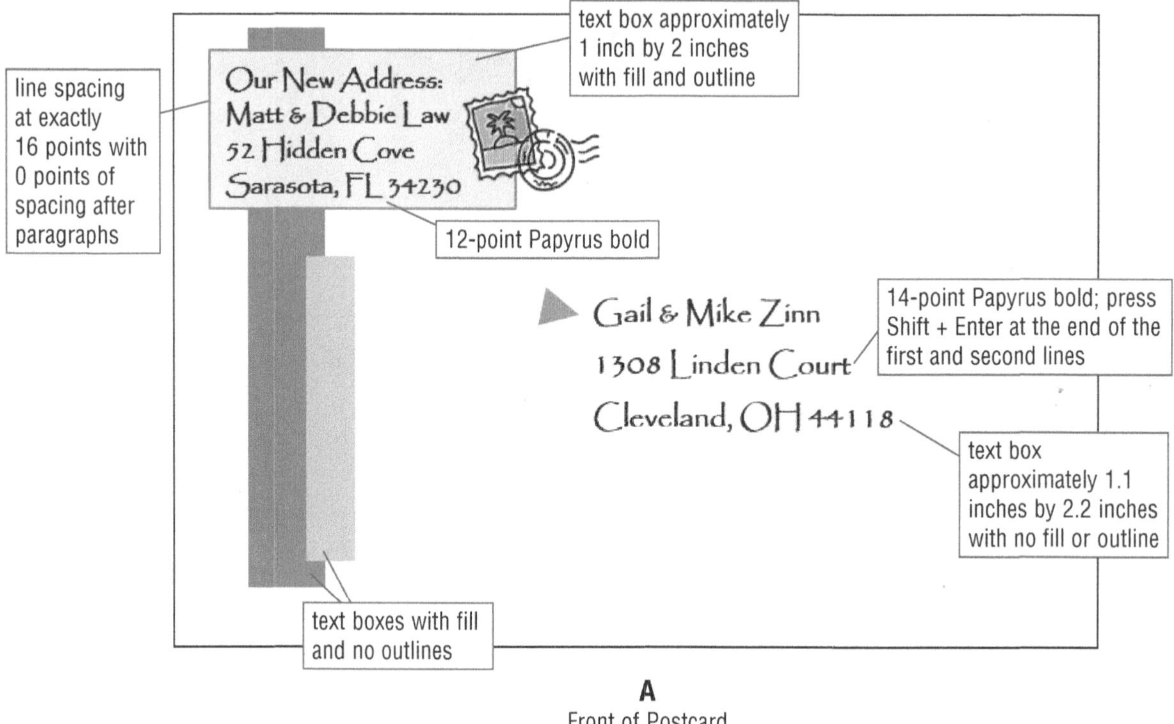

A
Front of Postcard

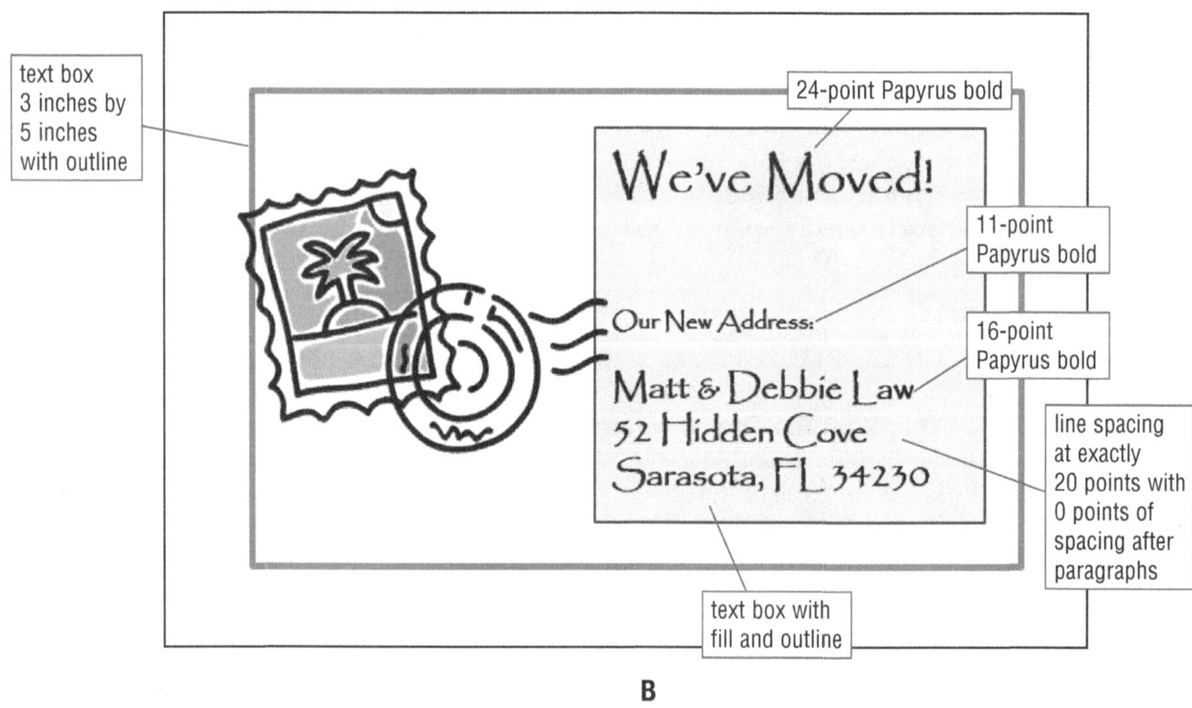

B
Back of Postcard

Assessment 2

Data Files

Create an Event Invitation

As a volunteer for a community outreach organization, you are responsible for creating an invitation that will be sent to the donors of the organization. Figure WB-3.2 shows one formatted invitation. You have been asked to use the same text but create the invitation with different formatting. Because the food and personal items are sorted and packaged in brown paper grocery bags for distribution, you will maintain this theme by using a brown paper bag as the envelope for your invitation. You will size the invitation to fit into a brown paper lunch bag, which measures approximately 5.5 inches by 10.5 inches. Complete the following steps to create the invitation:

1. At a blank document, change the size of the invitation by clicking the Layout tab, clicking the Size button, and then clicking *More Paper Sizes* at the drop-down list. At the Page Setup dialog box with the Paper tab selected, type 5 in the *Width* measurement box, type 10 in the *Height* measurement box, and then click OK.
2. Refer to Figure WB-3.2 for the text of the invitation, but create your invitation with different formatting than that shown in the figure.
3. Insert the **SOLogo.png** logo located in the C3 folder.
4. Save the document with the name **3-Volunteer**.
5. Print the invitation and trim the excess paper.
6. Close **3-Volunteer.docx**.
7. ***Optional:*** Insert the invitation into a brown paper lunch bag and then create a label to attach to the front of the bag using design elements similar to the ones you used for the invitation. Use the Avery US Label product number 6572 label. The label should include the text *You're invited! Look inside...* and include **grocerybag.png** located in the C3 folder.

Assessment 3

Data Files

Create a Hanging Name Tag and Agenda

As a virtual event planner, you run your business from your home. One of your clients, Global Network, is a network of accounting firms with members from all over the world. You are organizing an annual meeting for this group in Beijing in 2019. You have already prepared a template for the hanging name tags that the attendees will wear to all the activities. Along with the attendee's name, city, and country, the tag will include the conference agenda. Complete the following steps to format the hanging name tag and agenda, as shown in Figure WB-3.3 on page WB-19:

1. Open a document based on the template by completing the following steps:
   a. Open File Explorer.
   b. Navigate to the C3 folder.
   c. Double-click ***HangingNameTagTemplate.dotx***.
   d. Save the document with the name **3-HangingNameTag**.
2. Type the text for the front and back of the name tag as shown in Figure WB-3.3 and according to the specifications given in the figure:
   a. Use text boxes with the fill and outline removed, or type the text directly into the document, adjusting the line spacing by pressing the Enter key and adjusting the values in the *Before* and *After* measurement boxes in the *Spacing* section of the Paragraph dialog box. Consider adjusting the line spacing setting from the default *1.08* to *Single*, or type a value in the *Multiple*, *Exactly*, or *At least* measurement box at the Paragraph dialog box. Make sure to use any line or paragraph spacing recommendations displayed in the callouts shown in Figure WB-3.3.
   b. Click the logo on the front of the tag and then drag a copy of the logo to the back of the tag.

3. Type the agenda text for the inside left and inside right parts of the tag in the table cells of the template as shown in the figure:
   a. Use the tab settings shown in Figure WB-3.3.
   b. Insert en dashes in all the time durations.
4. Save **3-HangingNameTag.docx**.
5. Print one side of the document, reload the document into your printer, and then print the other side.
6. Trim the tag and fold it to fit into a clear plastic holder, if one is available.
7. Close **3-HangingNameTag.docx**.

Figure WB-3.2 Sample Invitation for Assessment 2

Figure WB-3.3 Name Tag and Agenda Created in Assessment 3

18-point Calibri bold italic

Embracing Change...

Drag and drop a copy of the logo from the back of the badge.

GLOBAL NETWORK
Beijing 2019

16-point Calibri bold, all caps

SEPTEMBER 16–17, 2019

PROGRAM

20-point Calibri bold, all caps

GLOBAL NETWORK
Beijing 2019

"Embracing Change" — 11-point Calibri bold

EDWARDO — 24-point Calibri bold, all caps

Perez — 20-point Calibri bold

Buenos Aires — 14-point Calibri bold

ARGENTINA — 20-point Calibri bold, all caps

Annual Meeting Program — 14-point Calibri bold

September 16–17, 2019 — 11-point Calibri italic

Select all the text in both text boxes and then change the line spacing to single spacing with no spacing after paragraphs.

9-point Calibri bold

Monday, September 16, 2019
DELEGATE'S PROGRAM

07:00–08:30	**Breakfast**	*Hall C*
08:30–09:00	**Opening Ceremony**	*Hall B*
09:00–09:30	**Welcome to Beijing** *Wang Xia, Chairman* *BDE Network (China)*	*Hall B*
09:30–10:45	**State of Accounting** *Dr. Liu Yu, Accounting Regulatory*	*Hall B*
10:45–11:00	**Coffee Break**	*Function Room Foyer*
11:00–11:30	**Overview of Meeting** *Frank B. Hartford, CEO*	*Hall B*
11:30–12:30	**Strategic Plan** *Robert DeLong, Chairman*	*Room B*
12:30–13:30	**Lunch**	*Room B*
13:30–14:30	**Building a Global Brand** *Professor Sue Ping, Northwest University*	*Conference Room B*
14:30–14:45	**Coffee Break**	*Function Room Foyer*
14:45–16:00	**Breakout Sessions**	*Function Rooms*
17:30–23:00	**Regional Dinners**	*Ristorante Sadler*

all caps

9-point Calibri

left tab at 0.8 inch

9-point Calibri italic

en dashes in all times

Tuesday, September 17, 2019
DELEGATE'S PROGRAM

07:00–08:30	**Breakfast**	*Room C*
08:30–10:30	**How to Help Clients Succeed & Win Business** *John Samuel, Burr Oak Group*	*Room B*
10:30–11:00	**Coffee Break**	*Function Room Foyer*
11:00–13:30	**Breakout Sessions**	*Function Rooms*
12:30–13:30	**Buffet Lunch** (in Breakout Rooms)	
13:30–14:30	**Awards & Recognition** *Frank B. Hartford, CEO*	*Hall B*
14:30–15:00	**Closing Comments** *Frank B. Hartford, CEO*	*Hall B*
15:00–15:15	**Coffee Break**	*Function Room Foyer*
15:15–16:00	**Celebrating 50 Years** *Frank B. Hartford, CEO*	*Hall B*
18:00–22:00	**Closing Dinner & Reception** **798 Art Zone** ***Buses depart from the West Conference Hall at 17:45***	
23:00–01:00	**Hospitality Suite**	*Function Room*

8-point Calibri italic

right tab at 2.9 inches

8-point Calibri bold

8-point Calibri bold italic

9-point Calibri bold

Assessment

Create and Format a Marketing Plan

INTEGRATED

GROUP PROJECT

As a team, create an attention-getting document advertising a spring promotion for a new line of products that your team chooses:

1. Apply styles, an appropriate theme, a background color, gradients, pictures, textures, or any other formatting elements to enhance the appearance of the document.
2. Save your document with the name **3-SpringPromotion**.
3. Print a copy of this document for each member of your class and then close the document.
4. Using PowerPoint, prepare a presentation to promote the line of products. Include at least five slides in the presentation. Save the presentation with the name **3-Products**. Print and then close **3-Products.pptx**.

Visual Benchmark

Data Files

Create a Certificate of Completion for a Course

1. At a blank document, search for a template using *certificate* as the search word. Double-click the template that is similar to what displays in Figure WB-3.4. (If this template is not available, open File Explorer, navigate to the C3 folder, and then double-click ***Certificate.dotx***.)
2. Format the certificate as shown in Figure WB-3.4, with the following specifications:
   a. Include your name as the certificate recipient, your course name as the program name, and the current date in the circle. ***Hint: Change the paragraph spacing before the month and day to* 6 pt *to better display the date.***
   b. Insert your instructor's name below the signature line and then delete the *[Signatory Title]* placeholder.
   c. Delete the logo text box in the lower right corner of the certificate and then insert **ribbon.png** from the C3 folder. Recolor, size, and position the ribbon as shown in the figure.
   d. Change any font colors as shown in the figure.
3. Save the completed certificate with the name **3-ClassCertificate**.
4. Print and then close **3-ClassCertificate.docx**.

Figure WB-3.4 Visual Benchmark Certificate

Case Study

Data Files

You work for Alpine Animal Center and one of your job responsibilities is to create a monthly calendar of the dates and times of upcoming classes and events. Open **AACCalendar.docx** and then save it with the name **3-AACCalendar**. Use the information you learned in this chapter about creating calendars to format the calendar. Include the following:

- Delete the image placeholder (box that contains an *X*) and then insert **pets.jpg** in the table cell.
- Insert **AACLogo.jpg** from the C3 folder and then size and position the logo anywhere in the calendar.
- Change the shading of the table cells to better match the logo colors.
- Include the following classes, dates, and times in the calendar:
  - o Puppy training class: every Monday from 6:30 to 7:30 p.m.
  - o Pet care class: May 23 from 6:00 to 7:00 p.m.
  - o Vaccine clinic: third Thursday of the month from 9:00 a.m. to 3:00 p.m.

Make any other necessary changes to enhance the appearance of the calendar. Save, print, and then close **3-AACCalendar.docx**.

Part 2

Dr. Marissa St. Blanc has asked you to create mailing labels for Alpine Animal Center. Use the center's mailing information (shown below) to create a sheet of mailing labels. You determine the style of mailing labels and include the center's logo on each label. ***Hint: Consider saving the label image and address to the Quick Part gallery to help quickly fill an entire sheet of labels.*** Save the labels document with the name **3-AACLabels**. Print and then close the document.

Alpine Animal Center
5015 Fourth Avenue
Kearney, NE 68875

Part 3

Data Files

Dr. St. Blanc has asked you to create a form template for class registration at Alpine Animal Center. In Word, open **AACClassForm.dotx** and then save it with the name **3-AACClassForm** in the C3 folder. Make sure the file is saved in the .dotx (template) format. Turn on Design mode, insert plain text content controls one space after the colon in each of rows three through seven in both columns, and then turn off Design mode. Change the shading of the cells, border colors, and font colors to better match the letterhead. Save, print, and then close **3-AACClassForm.dotx**. Open File Explorer, navigate to the C3 folder, and then double-click **3-AACClassForm.dotx**. (This opens a document based on the template.) Insert the following information in the content controls:

Owner name: Gerardo Florez
Street address: 5883 Cascade Drive
City, State, ZIP: Bend, OR 97702
Phone number: (541) 555-0121
Email address: gflorez@emcp.net

Pet name: Roscoe
Pet breed: German Sheppard
Pet gender: Male
Pet age: 4 months
Class name: Puppy Training

Save the completed form with the name **3-AACClassReg.docx**. Print and then close the form.

Part 4

Data Files

One of your responsibilities at the Alpine Animal Center is to create a certificate of completion for each pet that completes a training class. To streamline this task, you decide to create a certificate template that includes text content controls and date content controls. In Word, open **AACCertificate.dotx** and then save it with the name **3-AACCertificate** in the C3 folder. Make sure the file is saved in the .dotx (template) format. Insert **AACLogo.jpg** from the C3 folder into the certificate and then size and position the logo as desired. Turn on Design mode and then insert plain text content controls below the text *CERTIFICATE OF COMPLETION*, below the text *has successfully completed the*, and one space to the right of the colon after the text *PRESENTED BY*. Insert a date picker content control one space to the right of the colon after the text *ON THIS DAY* and then turn off Design mode. Save, print, and then close **3-AACCertificate.dotx**. Open File Explorer, navigate to the C3 folder, and then double-click **3-AACCertificate.dotx**. Create a certificate for Gracie completing the Puppy Training Class; the award will be presented to her by Sean Hudson on July 19, 2018. Save the certificate with the name **3-AACCertPuppy.docx**. Print and then close the certificate.

Creating Letterheads, Envelopes, Business Cards, and Press Releases

CHAPTER 4

Study Tools

Study tools include a presentation and a glossary. Use these resources to help you further develop and review skills learned in this chapter.

Concepts Check

Check your understanding by identifying application tools used in this chapter. If you are a SNAP user, launch the Concepts Check from your Assignments page.

Recheck

Check your understanding by taking this quiz. If you are a SNAP user, launch the Recheck from your Assignments page.

Skills Assessment

Assessment 1

Create and Use a Letterhead for a Foreign Hotel

Data Files

The Isar Hotel in Munich, Germany, has just opened and you are responsible for creating the hotel letterhead. Look at the letterhead in Figure WB-4.1 on page WB-25 and then create the letterhead and letter with the following specifications:

1. At a blank document, type WILLKOMMEN ZUM ☞ ISAR HOTEL MÜNICH as WordArt text using the Gradient Fill: Blue, Accent color 5; Reflection WordArt option, as shown in Figure WB-4.1. (Insert the *Ü* symbol at the Symbol dialog box with the (normal text) font selected [character code 00DC] and insert the ☞ symbol with the Wingdings font selected [character code 106].)
2. Select the WordArt text box containing the text you just typed and then make the following changes:
   a. Change the font to 11-point Segoe UI Semibold.
   b. Apply the Orange, Accent 2, Darker 50% font color.
   c. Expand the spacing of the text by 4.7 points. (Do this at the Font dialog box with the Advanced tab selected.)
   d. Align the WordArt text box above the address text box, as shown in Figure WB-4.1.
3. Insert a text box in the document and then type the hotel address (the character code for ü is 00FC) and phone and fax numbers, as shown in the figure. Press Shift + Enter and then type the web address. Select the text box and then apply the following formatting:
   a. Change the paragraph alignment to right.
   b. Change the font to 8-point Microsoft JhengHei and then apply bold formatting.
   c. Apply the Dark Blue font color.
   d. Select the web address, apply italic formatting, and then change the font size to 7 points.
   e. Remove the text box shape fill and outline.
   f. Size the text box to accommodate the text and then position the text box as shown in Figure WB-4.1.

4. Insert **IsarHotel.png** from the C4 folder and then apply the following formatting:
   a. Change the height of the image to 0.8 inch.
   b. Change the text wrapping to Tight.
   c. Position the image as shown in Figure WB-4.1 on page WB-25.
5. Select both text boxes and the image and then group the objects.
6. To change the position of the grouped objects, select the grouped image, click the Position button in the Arrange Group on the Picture Tools Format tab and then click *Position in Top Center with Square Text Wrapping* at the drop-down gallery.
7. Press Ctrl + End to move the insertion point below the grouped objects, click the Home tab, and then click the *No Spacing* style in the Styles group.
8. Save the document as a template in your C4 folder with the name **4-HotelLtrhd**.
9. Close **4-HotelLtrhd.dotx**.
10. Open File Explorer, navigate to the C4 folder, and then double-click **4-HotelLtrhd.dotx.** (This opens a document based on the template.)
11. Type text in the letter as shown in Figure WB-4.1. (Insert the *ä* in the word *Sächlich* at the Symbol dialog box with the (normal text) font selected [character code 00E4].)
12. Save the completed letter with the name **4-HotelLetter**.
13. Print and then close **4-HotelLetter.docx**.

Assessment 2

Data Files

Create an Envelope for the Hotel

Use some of the letterhead elements you created in Assessment 1 to create an envelope for the hotel (as shown in Figure WB-4.2 on page WB-26) with the following specifications:

1. Insert an envelope in a new, blank document.
2. Insert in the envelope **IsarHotel.png** from the C4 folder.
3. Change the height of the image to 0.9 inch.
4. Change the text wrapping to Tight.
5. Insert a text box with no fill and no outline. Type the hotel address in the text box (press Shift + Enter after typing the first line of the address), select the text you just typed, and then change the font to 9-point Microsoft JhengHei and apply the Dark Blue font color. Apply bold formatting and change the paragraph alignment to right.
6. Insert a text box with no fill and no outline and then type ISAR HOTEL MÜNICH.
7. Select the text you just typed and then apply the Gradient Fill: Blue, Accent color 5; Reflection text effect. (Use the Text Effects and Typography button in the Font group on the Home tab.)
8. With the text still selected, change the font to 11-point Segoe UI Semibold; change the font color to Orange, Accent 2, Darker 50%; and expand the character spacing of the text by 6 points.
9. Size and position the elements so your envelope is similar to the envelope in Figure WB-4.2.
10. Save the envelope document with the name **4-HotelEnvelope**.
11. Print and then close **4-HotelEnvelope.docx**. (It may be necessary to manually feed the envelope.)

Figure WB-4.1 Letterhead and Letter Created in Assessment 1

WILLKOMMEN ZUM & ISAR HOTEL MÜNICH

Wilenmayerstrade 10, 803 München, GERMANY, TEL +49 (0) 89 55544 0, FAX +49 (0) 89 55544 1000

www.isarhotel.emcp.net

Herzlich Willkommen Im Isar Sächlich Münich

May 14, 2018

Dear Guest,

I am very pleased that you have chosen Isar Hotel Münich for your stay in Münich.

As part of the Schöenfeld Luxury Hotels, we offer top-class surroundings for your stay. Our staff is dedicated to making your stay an enjoyable experience. Every Schöenfeld Hotel is uniquely designed for guests who expect excellence and value individuality. Whether your stay is a business-related event, a luxury holiday, or a relaxing vacation experience, we invite you to discover our chain of hotels.

Please contact us immediately, at any time, with any special requests, questions, or concerns. We want your stay to be luxurious and carefree.

I wish you a successful and enjoyable stay.

Sincerely,

Gerhard Kohl
General Manager

Figure WB-4.2 Envelope Created in Assessment 2

Assessment 3

Data Files

PORTFOLIO

Create Business Cards for the Hotel Manager

Create business cards for the general manager of the Isar Hotel as shown in Figure WB-4.3 with the following specifications:

1. At a blank document, insert blank labels using the *Avery US Letter* label vendor and the *8371 Business Cards* product number.
2. Insert **IsarHotel.png** in the first label, change the height of the image to 1.1 inches, apply Tight text wrapping, and then position the image as shown in Figure WB-4.3.
3. Create a text box for the hotel address, telephone number, and web address. Remove the text box shape fill and outline and then type the text in the text box as shown in Figure WB-4.3. Select the text you just typed, change the line spacing to Single, change the spacing after paragraphs to 0, change the font to 9-point Microsoft JhengHei, apply bold formatting, change the text color to Dark Blue, and change the paragraph alignment to right. Select the web address, change the font size to 8 points, and then apply italic formatting. Size and position the text box as shown in Figure WB-4.3.
4. Create a text box for the name and title, *Gerhard Kohl, General Manager*. Remove the text box shape fill and outline and then type Gerhard Kohl, General Manager. Select the text you just typed, change the font to 11-point Microsoft JhengHei, apply bold formatting, and change the font color to Dark Blue. Size and position the text box as shown in Figure WB-4.3.
5. Create WordArt using the Gradient Fill: Blue, Accent color 5; Reflection option. Type ISAR HOTEL MÜNICH in the WordArt text box. Select the text you just typed, change the font to 14-point Segoe UI Semibold, apply the Orange, Accent 2, Darker 50% font color, and expand the text by 6 points. Size and position the WordArt as shown in Figure WB-4.3.
6. Select the image, the two text boxes, and the WordArt text box and then group the objects. Save the grouped objects in the Quick Part gallery and name the quick part *XX-IsarHotel* (typing your initials in place of the *XX*).

7. Click the Mailings tab and then click the Labels button. At the Envelopes and Labels dialog box with the Labels tab selected, type XX-IsarHotel (typing your initials in place of the *XX*) in the *Address* text box, press the F3 function key, and then click the New Document button.
8. Save the labels document with the name **4-IHBusinessCards**.
9. Print and then close **4-IHBusinessCards.docx**.
10. Close the document containing the single label without saving the document.

Figure WB-4.3 Business Card Created in Assessment 3

Assessment

4

PORTFOLIO

Download Templates and Create a Letterhead and Business Cards

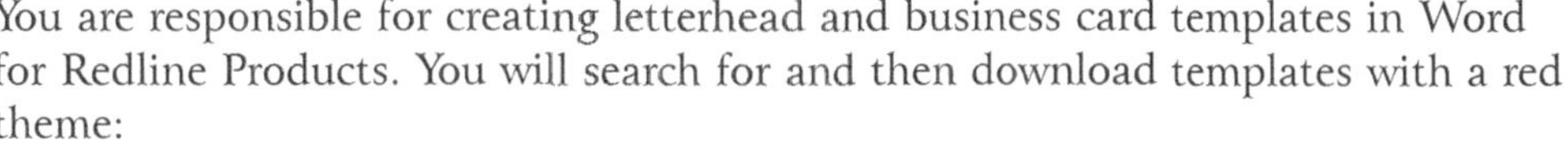

You are responsible for creating letterhead and business card templates in Word for Redline Products. You will search for and then download templates with a red theme:

1. In Word, search for and then download a letterhead template with a red theme. Use the company name, *Redline Products*, and then fill in the remaining placeholders in the letterhead with information of your choosing. Save the completed letterhead as a template in your C4 folder with the name **4-RPLetterhead**. Print and then close the letterhead template.
2. In Word, search for and then download a business card template with a red theme. Insert the appropriate information in the placeholders using the same information you inserted in the letterhead. Save the completed business card as a template in the C4 folder and name it **4-RPBusinessCards**. Print and then close the business card template.

Assessment

5

GROUP PROJECT

Design Documents for a Hotel

As a group project, create a fictitious hotel in a city that interests you. For this hotel, prepare the following documents:

1. At a blank document, create an attractive and well-designed letterhead. Save the letterhead as a template with the name **4-LtrhdTemplate**. Print and then close **4-LtrhdTemplate.dotx**.
2. Open a document based on the letterhead template your team created and then type a document that includes a SmartArt graphic that provides information to guests on times for check-in, continental breakfast, afternoon snack, and check-out. Figure WB-4.4 illustrates a sample solution. Save the completed document with the name **4-HotelInfo**. Print and then close **4-HotelInfo.docx**.

3. Use the Internet to search for points of interest in and around the city you have chosen for your hotel. Create a document sheet with information about at least five points of interest. Figure WB-4.5 illustrates a sample solution. Include a predesigned text box, use WordArt text, and consider design elements such as clip art, photographs, and design themes when creating your document. Save the completed document with the name **4-PointsofInterest**. Print and then close **4-PointsofInterest.docx**.

Figure WB-4.4 Sample Information Sheet for Assessment 5, Step 2

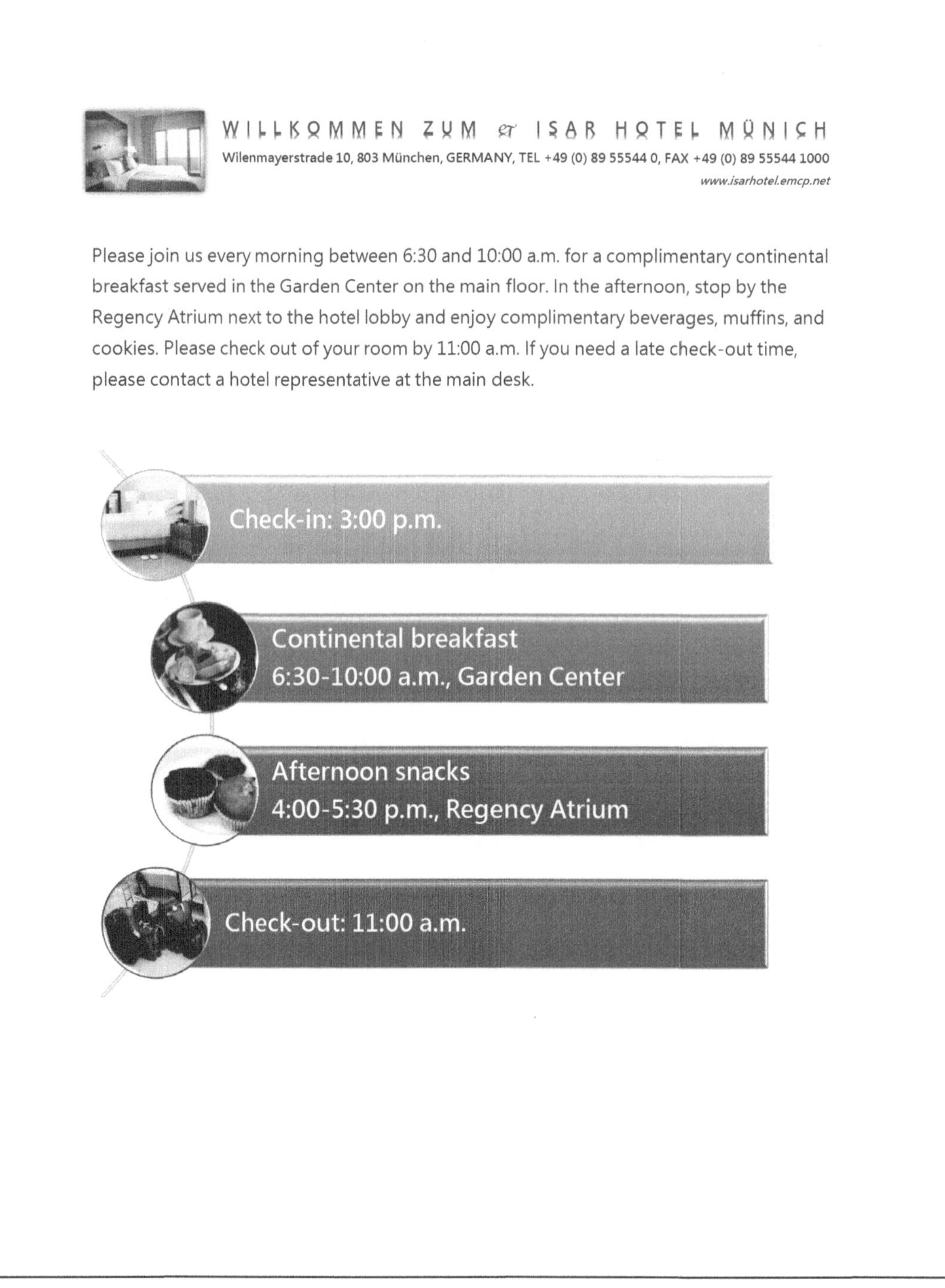

Figure WB-4.5 Sample Information Sheet for Assessment 5, Step 3

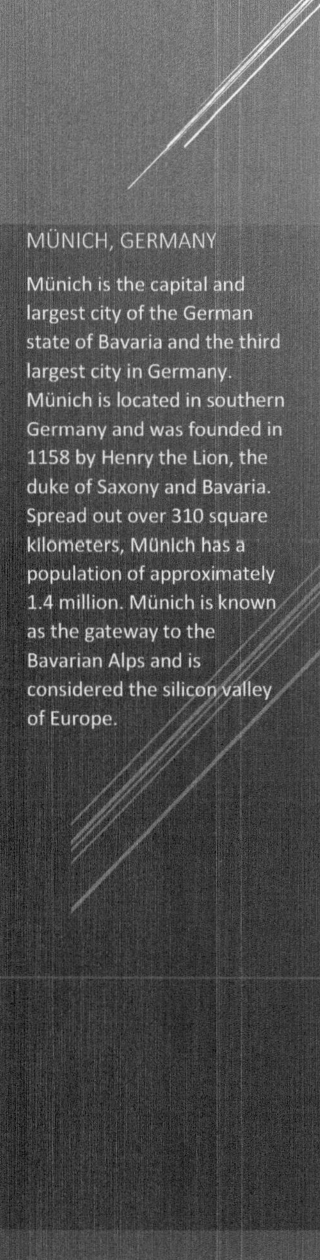

MÜNICH

Marienplatz

Marienplatz is the central square in the center of Münich. In the square, you can explore a variety of buildings, churches, and landmarks. Mariensäule, the Marian Column topped with the golden statue of the Virgin Mary, is located in Marienplatz.

The English Garden

Münich's largest park, The English Garden, is a wonderful place to explore. The park provides a variety of recreational activities—rent a paddle boat, stroll along the wooded paths, and visit a traditional beer garden.

Residence Palace of Münich

The Residence Palace lies at the edge of Münich's old town and is the former royal palace of the Bavarian monarchs. Today the Residence houses one of the best European museums of interior decoration.

Deutsches Museum

The Deutsches Museum is located on an island in the Isar river that runs through Münich's city center. The museum is one of the oldest and largest science and technology museums in the world and boasts an impressive collection of historic artifacts.

Olympic Stadium

The site for the 1972 Summer Olympics, the Olympic Stadium was revolutionary and futuristic for its time. The transparent canopies of acrylic glass, modeled after the Alps, are the signature characteristic of the stadium.

http://en-wikipedia.org/wiki/Munich
http://gogermany.about.com/od/citiesandregions/tp/Munich

Visual Benchmark

Format a Press Release

Data Files

1. Open **JJMPressRelease.docx** and then save it with the name **4-JJMPressRelease**.
2. Format the press release so it appears as shown in Figure WB-4.6 with the following specifications:
   a. Insert the image **jojomart.png** from the C4 folder.
   b. Use the Arial Narrow font for the contact information and titles, use the Arial font for the body text, and use various font sizes that approximately match the type shown in Figure WB-4.6.
   c. Create a custom footer, as shown in Figure WB-4.6.
3. Save, print, and then close **4-JJMPressRelease.docx**.

Figure WB-4.6 Visual Benchmark

FOR IMMEDIATE RELEASE
April 20, 2018
Contact: Jebediah Townsly
JoJo-Mart
310 Kingsford Street
Quarth, WI 54484
www.jojomart.emcp.net
Phone: (608) 555-1937

PRESS RELEASE

JoJo-Mart Introduces Local Organic Produce
Local organics will be available this summer.

Quarth, April 20, 2018: This summer, JoJo-Mart, the provider of farm fresh produce and other foods, is going to offer a wide variety of local organic produce. All organics have been certified through the OrgaCert Association, which test for GMO, pesticides, and other synthetic materials.

Due to a large number of requests, JoJo-Mart has started contacting local farmers about organic produce. There was a very positive response from the farmers, who work hard to keep their crops organic. This summer, JoJo-Mart will be offering these organic foods in a newly designated area of the store. On the weekends, the outdoor market will also include many organic offerings, so come down and check it out.

If you would like to learn more, contact Jebediah Townsly at jebtown@emcp.net. Also, visit the website www.jojo-mart.emcp.net to request certain organic items! Click the Request Form link in the upper-right corner to begin a request. The website also contains a list of all the organic farmers that will supply JoJo-Mart.

###

FOR IMMEDIATE RELEASE April 20, 2018

Case Study

Part 1

Data Files

You are the assistant to Paul Brewster, the marketing coordinator at NorthWest Aviation, a medium-sized flight school. You have been asked by Mr. Brewster to prepare new business documents that will be used for mailing and contacting people. Mr. Brewster has already created the Word document **NWAInfo.docx**, which includes all the information and company graphics. Open **NWAInfo.docx** and save it with the name **4-NWALetterhead.docx**. Use the graphics and information to create a letterhead. If desired, further customize the letterhead by using additional images and graphic elements. Use any of the Word 2016 elements you have learned in Chapter 4 to enhance the design of the letterhead. Save and then print **4-NWALetterhead.docx**.

Part 2

Using the letterhead you created for NorthWest Aviation in Part 1, create and add an envelope to **4-NWALetterhead.docx**. Insert the envelope using the Envelope feature on the Mailings tab. Use the design elements and information you created or customized in Part 1 to create the envelope. Save the document with the name **4-NWALetterhead+Envelope**. Print and then close **4-NWALetterhead+Envelope.docx**.

Part 3

Using the design elements, graphics, and information you created for NorthWest Aviation in Parts 1 and 2, create a sheet of business cards using the labels feature. Choose the correct paper manufacturer and code for your system. (If unknown, use *US Avery Letter, 8371 Business Cards*.) Save the document with the name **4-NWABusinessCards**. Print and then close **4-NWABusinessCards.docx**.

Part 4

Data Files

The identity and style of NorthWest Aviation business documents have been established in the previous parts of the case study. Mr. Brewster would like to send out a press release that he has written using the new identity and style you have created. At a blank document, begin creating a press release by copying elements from the other company documents and pasting them into the blank document. Make sure to include all the vital contact information near the top, and use Paul Brewster as the contact person. Once the graphics and contact information are in place, insert the text from **NWAPressRelease.docx** using the Objects button on the Insert tab. Create a custom footer that includes at least the current date. Save the document with the name **4-NWAPressRelease**. Print and then close **4-NWAPressRelease.docx.**

Unit 1 Performance Assessment

Assessing Proficiency

In this unit, you have learned about important desktop publishing concepts, as well as how to plan and design documents based on design principles that include focus, balance, proportion, contrast, color, directional flow, and consistency. You have also learned to apply design concepts to create personal documents, letterheads, envelopes, business cards, press releases.

Data Files

Before beginning unit work, copy the U1 folder to your storage medium and then make U1 the active folder.

Assessment 1

Data Files

Create an Invitation

1. Open **SpringGala.docx** and then save it with the name **U1-SpringGala**.
2. Create a text box for the text in Figure WB-U1.1. Remove the shape fill and shape outline from the text box.
3. Type the text shown in the text box in Figure WB-U1.1 (except for the ampersand [&] between *Spring Gala* and *Charity Ball*). Insert an en dash between *7:30 p.m.* and *Midnight*.
4. Select *Spring Gala* and *Charity Ball* and then make the following changes:
   a. Change the font to 60-point Gabriola.
   b. Apply the Fill: Black, Text color 1; Outline: White, Background color 1; Hard Shadow: Blue, Accent color 5 text effect (second column, bottom row).
   c. Change the text fill to Blue, Accent 1, Darker 50%.
   d. Display the Font dialog box with the Advanced tab selected, expand the character spacing by 1 point, apply stylistic set 6, and then close the dialog box.
   e. Change the spacing after paragraphs to 12 points.
5. Select the remaining text, change the font to 16-point Harrington, change the font color to Blue, Accent 1, Darker 50%, apply bold formatting, and then expand the spacing by 1 point.
6. Create a second text box and then remove the shape fill and shape outline.
7. Type an ampersand (&) inside the text box, select the ampersand, and then make the following changes:
   a. Change the font to 72-point Vivaldi.
   b. Apply the Fill: White; Outline: Blue, Accent color 5; Shadow text effect (fourth column, first row).
   c. Apply the Green, Accent 6, Lighter 60% text fill.
   d. Position the ampersand as shown in Figure WB-U1.1.
8. Make any other necessary changes so that your document appears similar to the document in Figure WB-U1.1.
9. Save, print, and then close **U1-SpringGala.docx**.

Figure WB-U1.1 Invitation Created in Assessment 1

Assessment 2

Format a Memo

1. Open **CMHMemo.docx** and then save it with the name **U1-CMHMemo**.
2. Format the memo so it appears as shown in Figure WB-U1.2 with the following specifications:
   a. With the insertion point positioned at the beginning of the document, insert **CMHLogo.png** from the U1 folder. Change the text wrapping to Behind Text.
   b. Change the *e* in the name *Medard* to *é* using a symbol from the Symbol dialog box with the (normal text) font selected.
   c. Select the text *(Current Date)* and then type the current date.
   d. Apply bullet formatting to the paragraphs as shown in the figure.
   e. Select the two hyphens between the words *signed* and *admissions* in the first bulleted paragraph and then insert an em dash.

f. Insert the text box containing the word *CONFIDENTIAL*. Change the height of the text box to 0.5 inch and the width to 2 inches and then apply the Blue, Accent 5, Darker 25% shape fill.
g. Change the font for the word *CONFIDENTIAL* in the text box to 14-point Arial Black and then apply the White, Background 1 font color. Remove the extra spacing after paragraphs in the text box and change the line spacing to Single. Center the text horizontally and vertically in the text box. ***Hint: Use the Align Text button in the Text group on the Drawing Tools Format tab to vertically center the text.***
h. Change the position of the text box to Position in Bottom Right with Square Text Wrapping.

3. Save, print, and then close **U1-CMHMemo.docx**.

Figure WB-U1.2 Memo Formatted in Assessment 2

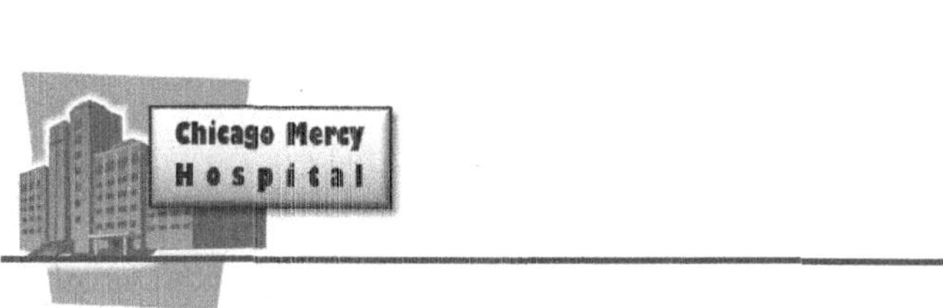

TO: Fred Médard

FROM: Juliette Danner

DATE: (Current Date)

SUBJECT: PREOPERATIVE PROCEDURES

At the meeting of the medical team, concern was raised about the structure of preoperative procedures. Due to that concern, the team decided to review written procedures to determine if additional steps should be added. A meeting of the surgical team has been set for Tuesday, May 29. Please try to arrange surgical schedules so a majority of the surgical team can attend this meeting.

Please review the following items to determine where each should be positioned in a preoperative surgical checklist:

- Necessary operative forms are signed—admissions and consent for surgery.
- Blood tests have been completed.
- Blood type is noted in patient chart.
- Surgical procedure has been triple-checked with patient and surgical team.
- All allergies are noted in patient chart.
- Anesthesiologist has reviewed and initialed patient chart.

I am confident that the medical team will discover that the preoperative checklist is one of the most thorough in the region. Any suggestions made by the medical team will only enhance a superior checklist.

xx: U1-CMHMemo.docx

CONFIDENTIAL

Assessment 3

Data Files

Create and Save an Agenda as a Template

1. Open **CMHAgenda.docx** and then save it with the name **U1-CMHAgenda**.
2. Insert the image **CMHLogo.png** from the U1 folder. Change the height of the image to 1.9 inches and change the position to Position in Top Left with Square Text Wrapping.
3. Move the insertion point to the end of the document and then create a table with three columns and seven rows.
4. Select the entire table and then apply the following formatting:
   a. Apply the List Table 6 Colorful - Accent 5 table style (sixth column, sixth row in the *List Tables* section).
   b. Change the font to 11-point Arial and then apply the Blue, Accent 1, Darker 50% font color.
   c. Change the row height to 0.7 inch.
   d. Select all of the cells in the table and then click the Align Center Left button in the Alignment group on the Table Tools Layout tab.
5. Select the first row of the table and then apply center alignment to the cells.
6. Click in the first cell in the first column and type Time, click in the first cell of the second column and type Topic, and then click in the first cell of the third column and type Discussion Leader.
7. Select the text you just typed in the first row, change the font size to 14 points, and then apply the small caps effect.
8. Save **U1-CMHAgenda.docx**.
9. Save the document as a template (in the .dotx file format) in the U1 folder and name the template **U1-CMHAgendaTemplate**.
10. Close **U1-CMHAgendaTemplate.dotx**.
11. Using File Explorer, open a document based on **U1-CMHAgendaTemplate.dotx**.
12. Type text in the document as shown in Figure WB-U1.3. (Insert en dashes between the times in the first column and insert the *ë* in the name *Zoë* at the Symbol dialog box.)
13. Save the completed agenda document with the name **U1-QCProjAgenda**.
14. Print and then close **U1-QCProjAgenda.docx**.

Assessment 4

Data Files

Use a Template to Create a Certificate

1. Open File Explorer, navigate to the U1 folder, and then double-click **SOCertificate.dotx**. (This opens a document based on the template.)
2. Modify the award certificate as shown in Figure WB-U1.4 by completing the following steps:
   a. Type the text in the placeholders. (Use your name in place of *Student Name*.)
   b. Insert **SOLogo.png** from the U1 folder, change the text wrapping of the image to In Front of Text, change the height to 1 inch, and then position the image as shown in the figure.
3. Save the completed certificate with the name **U1-SOCertificate**.
4. Print and then close **U1-SOCertificate.docx**.

Figure WB-U1.3 Agenda Created in Assessment 3

Chicago Mercy Hospital
Quality Care Projects
November 5
9:00 a.m. to Noon
Conference Room 8

AGENDA

TIME	TOPIC	DISCUSSION LEADER
9:00 a.m.–9:30 a.m.	Call to order and introduction of new project members	Becky Peterson, Chair
9:30 a.m.–10:00 a.m.	Presentation of project mission statement	Charles Visconti
10:00 a.m.–11:00 a.m.	Determination of project goals and timelines	Katrina O'Dell, Zoë Benn, and Wendy Mitaki
11:00 a.m.–11:45 a.m.	Brainstorming on public relations activities	Becky Peterson, Chair
11:45 a.m.–Noon	Scheduling of next project meeting	Becky Peterson, Chair
Noon	Adjournment	Becky Peterson, Chair

Figure WB-U1.4 Certificate Created in Assessment 4

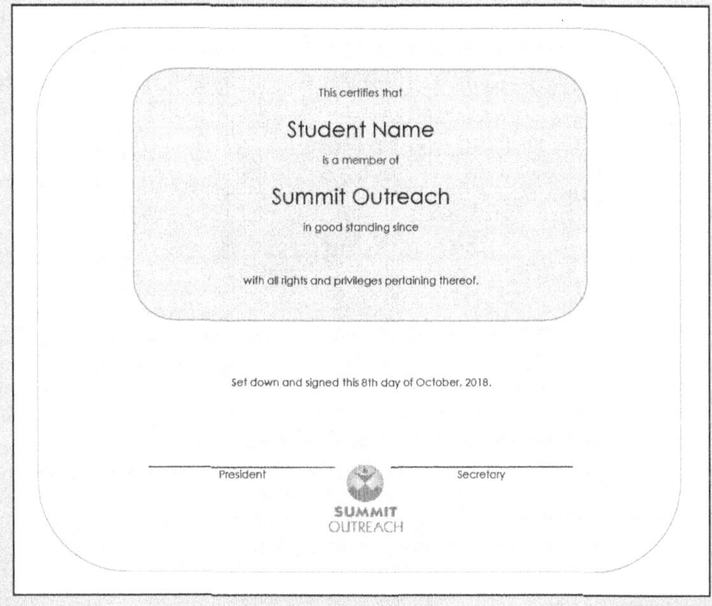

This certifies that

Student Name

is a member of

Summit Outreach

in good standing since

with all rights and privileges pertaining thereof.

Set down and signed this 8th day of October, 2018.

President

Secretary

SUMMIT
OUTREACH

Assessment

5

Data Files

Create a Letterhead and Envelope

1. At a blank document, create a letterhead similar to the one shown in Figure WB-U1.5 by completing the following steps:
   a. Insert, size, format, and position the image **eagle.png**, located in the U1 folder, as shown in Figure WB-U1.5.
   b. Create the *Blue Eagle Airlines* WordArt using the Fill: Black, Text color 1; Outline: White, Background color 1; Hard Shadow: Blue, Accent color 5 WordArt style, apply the Cascade: Up transform effect, and then change the font size to 24 points.
   c. Draw a text box and then type On the Wings of Eagles in 13-point Book Antiqua (substitute another font if necessary), apply italic formatting, expand the text by 1.5 points, and turn on kerning at 13 points and above. Change the font color to a color that coordinates with the eagle image and then remove the shape fill and shape outline from the text box. Position the text box as shown in the figure.
   d. Create the blue arrow extending from the image to the text box containing *On the Wings of Eagles*.
   e. Create a text box that contains the name *Dallas Love Field* set in 10-point Book Antiqua with bold formatting and blue font color and then add the following address information in 9-point Book Antiqua (substitute a different font if necessary):

      22 Mockingbird Lane
      Dallas, TX 75235
      emcp.net/beair
      214.555.6073
      1.800.555.6033
      214.555.6077 (Fax)

   f. Change the paragraph alignment in the text box to right. Adjust the line spacing and color as desired and then position the text box as shown in Figure WB-U1.5.
   g. Create another arrow that extends from *Eagles* to the text box containing the address, as shown in Figure WB-U1.5. Use the same arrow style and color used in the figure. (Both arrows in the document should be the same style and color.)
2. Create a coordinating envelope using the company name, address, and contact information as shown in Figure WB-U1.5 by completing the following steps:
   a. To add an envelope to the document, display the Envelopes and Labels dialog box with the Envelopes tab selected and then click the Add to Document button.
   b. Insert the letterhead graphics in the envelope by copying and pasting and then resize the graphics as necessary to fit the envelope.
   c. Add **stamp.png** to the envelope and then change the color of the image to match the color scheme of the envelope.
3. Save the completed letterhead and envelope document with the name **U1-BEAirlines**.
4. Print and then close **U1-BEAirlines.docx**.

Figure WB-U1.5 Letterhead and Envelope Created in Assessment 5

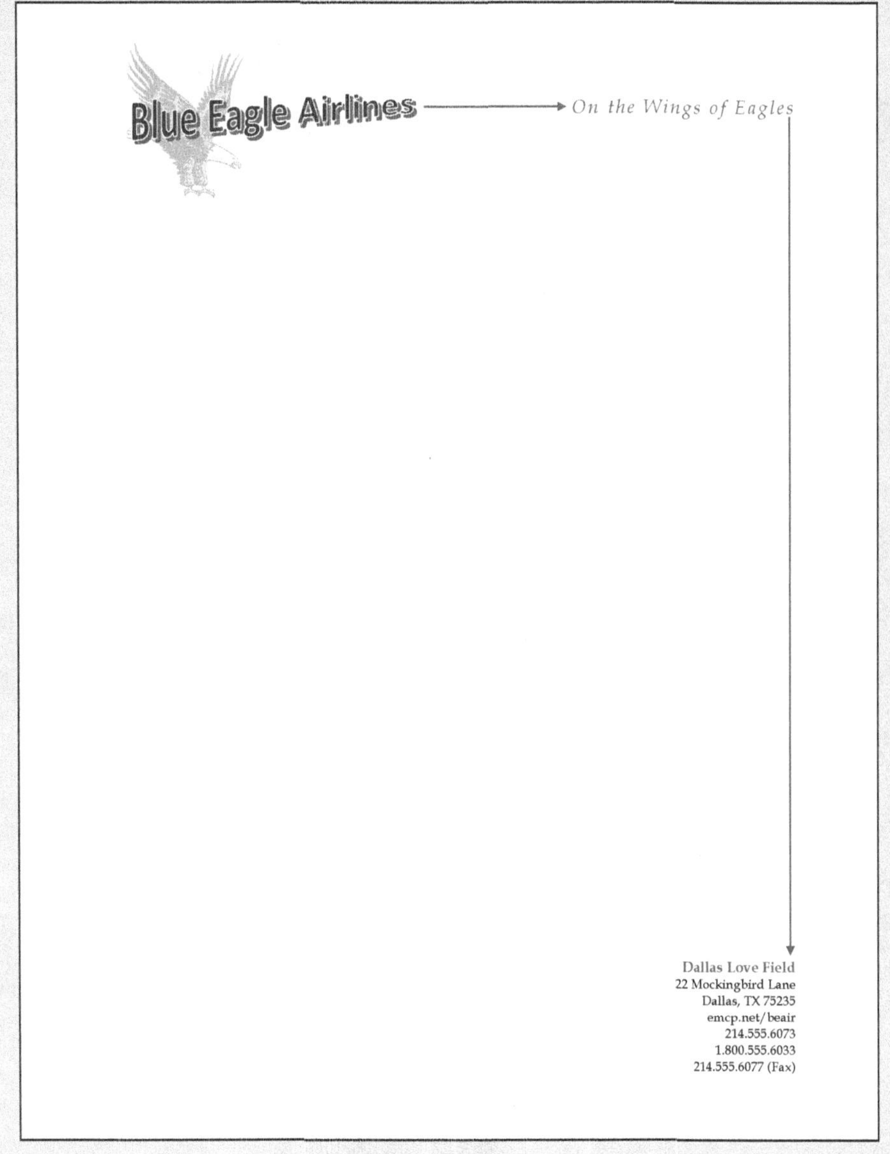

Assessment

6

Data Files

PORTFOLIO

Create a Business Card

1. At a blank document, insert Avery US Letter 8371 Business Cards labels. ***Hint: Use the Labels button in the Create group on the Mailings tab.***
2. In the first label on the sheet, create the business card shown in Figure WB-U1.6 by completing the following steps:
   a. Insert **SOLogo.png** at the left side of the cell, change the height to 1.5 inches, change the text wrapping to Square, and then position the image as shown in the figure.
   b. Create a text box for the information about Cindy Lopez. Format the text in the text box so it appears similar to what is shown in Figure WB-U1.6. (Use the Calibri font for the text.)
   c. Create a text box for the slogan *"We rise by lifting others."* Apply formatting so that the text appears similar to what is shown in Figure WB-U1.6 and then position the text box.
3. Group the logo and the two text boxes in the label and then save the grouped object as a quick part named **XX-SOBusinessCard**. (Use your initials in place of the *XX*.)
4. Save the label document with the name **U1-SOBusCardLabel** and then close the document.
5. At a blank document, display the Envelopes and Labels dialog box with the Labels tab selected, make sure the Avery US Letter, 8371 Business Cards label is selected in the *Label* section, type XX-SOBusinessCard in the *Address* list box (type your initials in place of the *XX*), press the F3 function key, and then click the New Document button.
6. Save the business cards document and name it **U1-SOBusCards**.
7. Print and then close **U1-SOBusCards.docx**.

Figure WB-U1.6 Business Card Created in Assessment 6

Assessment 7

Create the Back Side of a Business Card

1. Use Avery US Letter 8371 Business Cards labels to create the back sides of the business cards you created in Assessment 6. Add the text *Be a part of it!* and *Volunteer today at Summit Outreach* to the label. Include any additional elements you think will enhance the appearance of the card. You determine the formatting and positioning of the elements on the label.
2. Group the elements in the label and then save the grouped object as a quick part named **XX-SOBusCardBack**. (Use your initials in place of the *XX*.)
3. Save the label document with the name **U1-SOBusCardBackLabel** and then close the document.
4. At a blank document, create a sheet of Avery US Letter 8371 Business Cards labels and then insert the **XX-SOBusCardBack** quick part.
5. Save the business cards document and name it **U1-SOBusCardsBack**.
6. Print and then close **U1-SOBusCardsBack.docx**.

Assessment 8

Data Files

Insert a PowerPoint Slide into a Document

1. Create the memo shown in Figure WB-U1.7 with the following specifications:
   a. Display the New backstage area, then search for and download the Memo (Professional design) online template. (If this template is not available, choose a similar template.)
   b. Insert the text in the memo as shown in Figure WB-U1.7. ***Note: Your text may wrap differently than what displays in Figure WB-U1.7 if you used a different memo than specified in Step 1a.***
   c. Insert the PowerPoint slide in the memo by opening PowerPoint and then opening the presentation named **Presentation.pptx** located in the U1 folder. Click the slide in the slide thumbnails pane, copy the slide, make Word the active program, and then paste the slide into the memo document. Size and position the slide in the memo document as shown in the figure.
   d. Make any other necessary changes so your document appears similar to Figure WB-U1.7.
2. Save the document with the name **U1-PresMemo**.
3. Print and then close **U1-PresMemo.docx**.
4. Make PowerPoint active, close **Presentation.pptx**, and then close PowerPoint.

Figure WB-U1.7 Memo Created in Assessment 8

Leading Edge Consultants, Inc.

Memo

To: Dr. Carl Wilhelm

From: Tasha Slavinski

cc: Yasmin Rohan

Date: April 2, 2018

Re: PowerPoint Presentation

I have prepared the title slide for your presentation at the 2018 annual meeting at Casa De Campo in the Dominican Republic. Please review the PowerPoint slide shown below and let me know if you approve of the design. After you have approved the design, I will complete the remainder of the presentation and have it available for you by tomorrow.

U1-PresMemo.docx

DTP Challenge

Take your skills to the next level by completing these more challenging assessments.

Assessment

9

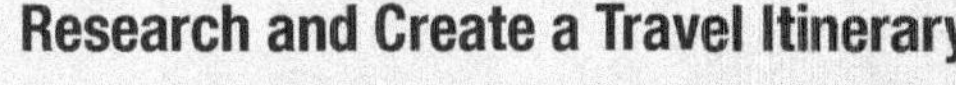

Research and Create a Travel Itinerary

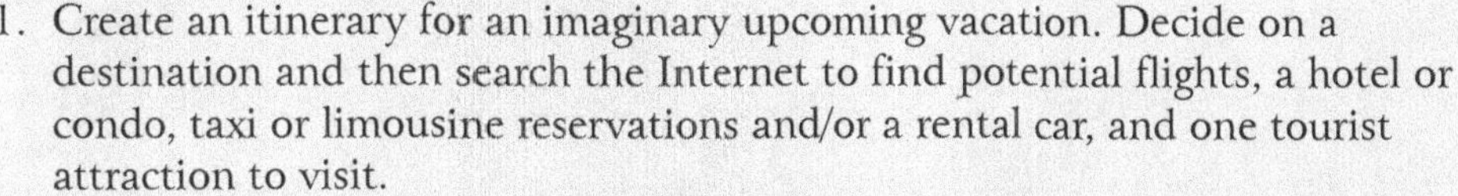

1. Create an itinerary for an imaginary upcoming vacation. Decide on a destination and then search the Internet to find potential flights, a hotel or condo, taxi or limousine reservations and/or a rental car, and one tourist attraction to visit.
2. Refer to a current style reference manual for information on how to format an itinerary, and consider arranging the information in a table. Organize your itinerary by dates and activities. Include all the pertinent times, addresses, and telephone numbers. Include the following information:
   a. Flight information: Airline name, flight number, departure time, arrival time, departure and arrival terminals, and seat number
   b. Hotel information: Hotel name, confirmation number, phone number, fax number, check-in date and time, and check-out date and time
   c. Transportation information: Rental car, taxi, or limousine name, telephone number, confirmation number, pick-up date and time, and return pick-up date and time
   d. Tour information, if relevant: Tour company name, destination, pick-up date and time, and telephone number
3. Add any other pertinent information about the trip.
4. Save the document with the name **U1-ItinChallenge**.
5. Print and then close **U1-ItinChallenge.docx**.

Assessment

10

Research and Create Files for a New Business

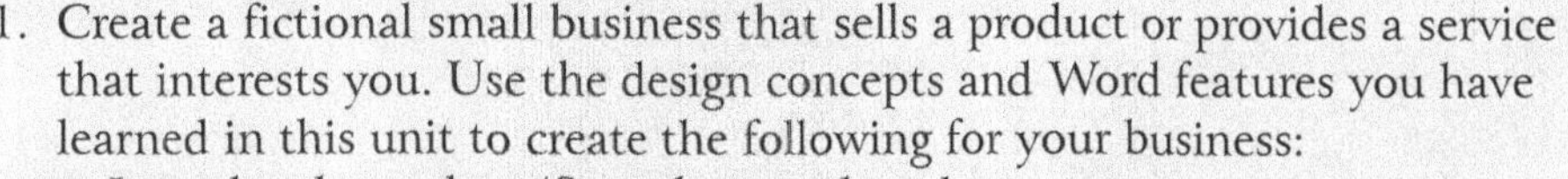

1. Create a fictional small business that sells a product or provides a service that interests you. Use the design concepts and Word features you have learned in this unit to create the following for your business:
   - Letterhead template (Save the template document as **LtrhdTemplate.dotx**.)
   - Envelope (Save the envelope document as **BusEnv.docx**.)
   - Business cards (Save the business cards document as **BusCards.docx**.)
2. Save each of the files you create and then print and close the files.
3. Using the **LtrhdTemplate.dotx** template you created, prepare a press release announcing the grand opening of your business. Include information such as dates and times, address, and contact numbers.
4. Save the press release and name it **U1-PressRelease**.
5. Print and then close **U1-PressRelease.docx**.

Microsoft®

Word Desktop Publishing

Unit 2

Preparing Business and Promotional Documents

Creating Flyers and Announcements

CHAPTER 5

Study Tools

Study tools include a presentation and a glossary. Use these resources to help you further develop and review skills learned in this chapter.

Concepts Check

Check your understanding by identifying application tools used in this chapter. If you are a SNAP user, launch the Concepts Check from your Assignments page.

Recheck

Check your understanding by taking this quiz. If you are a SNAP user, launch the Recheck from your Assignments page.

Skills Assessment

Assessment 1

Create a Community Announcement

1. At a blank document, insert **colorfulsun.jpg** from the C5 folder.
2. Make the following changes to the image:
   a. Apply Tight text wrapping.
   b. Click the Copy button.
   c. Use the Crop button on the Picture Tools Format tab to crop off the bottom half of the image.
   d. Deselect the image.
3. Click the Paste button to paste a copy of the original sun into the document and then make the following changes:
   a. Crop off the top half of the copy to the point at which you cropped off the bottom half of the original.
   b. Click the Color button in the Adjust group and then click the *Washout* option in the *Recolor* section.
4. Use the Align Objects button on the Picture Tools Format tab to center-align the top image and then the bottom image. Make any necessary adjustments to the images so they display as shown in Figure WB-5.1.
5. Draw a text box that measures 6.75 inches in height and 6.25 inches in width. Center the top of the text box with the top of the lightened part of the image. ***Hint: The sun should appear to be peeking over the text box.***
6. Remove the shape fill from the text box.
7. Use the *Dashes* option at the Shape Outline button drop-down gallery to add a round dotted orange border to the text box, and use the *Weight* option to increase the ruled line weight to 4½ points.
8. With the insertion point positioned in the text box, insert **GoodMorning.docx** from the C5 folder.

9. Select the text box, change the font to Tekton Pro, and then change the font color to Blue, Accent 5, Darker 50%. ***Note: If the Tekton Pro font is not available, substitute with Arial font.***
10. Select the text *Good Morning Naperville*, change the font size to 40 points, expand the spacing by 0.3 point, and turn on kerning for text 40 points and above.
11. Insert white space between the groups of text as shown in Figure WB-5.1. Make sure the text appears in the text box as shown in the figure. If necessary, adjust the size of the text box. ***Hint: Adjust the spacing using specific line spacing options or insert additional spacing before and after each paragraph with the* Before *and* After *measurement boxes in the Paragraph group on the Layout tab.***
12. Save the document with the name **5-GoodMorning**.
13. Print and then close **5-GoodMorning.docx**.

Figure WB-5.1 Announcement Created in Assessment 1

Assessment 2

Data Files

Create a Heart Health Flyer

1. At a blank document, change the page orientation to landscape.
2. Insert **heart.png** (see Figure WB-5.2) from the C5 folder and then apply the following formatting:
   a. Change the image width to 9 inches.
   b. Change the image position to Position in Middle Center with Square Text Wrapping.
   c. Change the text wrapping to Behind Text.
   d. Apply the Blur artistic effect.
3. Insert the text *Heart Attack Risk Factors* as WordArt text with the following specifications:
   a. Use the Fill: White; Outline: Blue, Accent color 1; Glow: Blue, Accent color 1 WordArt style (fourth column, second row).
   b. Apply the Square transform effect.
   c. Change the height to 0.5 inch.
   d. Position the WordArt as shown in Figure WB-5.2.
4. Insert the text *Groves Memorial Hospital* as WordArt text with the following specifications:
   a. Use the Fill: White; Outline: Blue, Accent color 1; Glow: Blue, Accent color 1 WordArt style (fourth column, second row).
   b. Change the font size of the WordArt text to 18 points.
   c. Position the WordArt as shown in Figure WB-5.2.
5. Insert a text box and then modify it with the following specifications:
   a. Change the height to 4.7 inches and the width to 4.3 inches.
   b. Change the position to Position in Middle Center with Square Text Wrapping.
   c. Apply the Subtle Effect - Blue, Accent 1 shape style (second column, fourth row in the *Theme Styles* section).

Figure WB-5.2 Flyer Created in Assessment 2

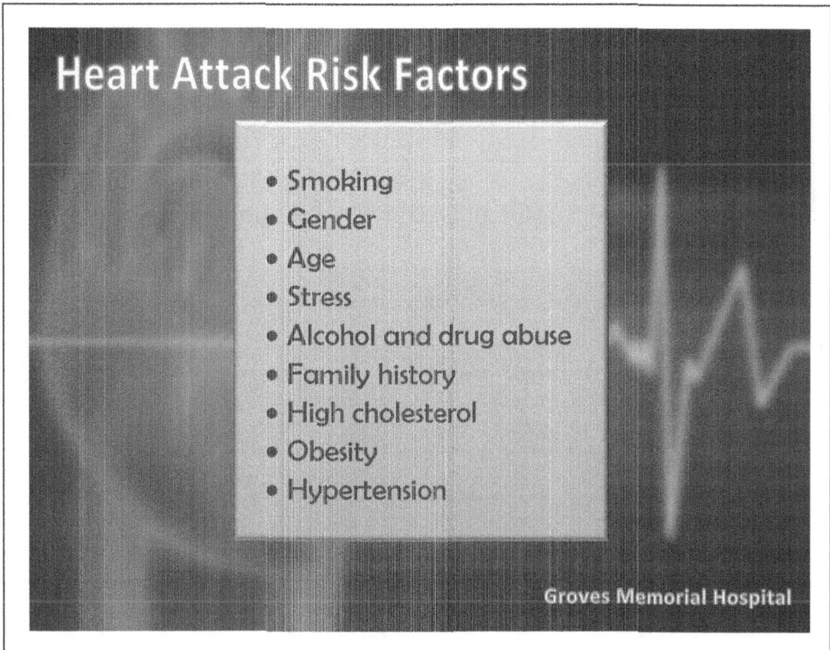

d. Apply the Round bevel effect. ***Hint: Do this at the Shape Effects button drop-down list.***
e. Position the insertion point inside the text box and then insert **RiskFactors.docx** from the C5 folder.
f. Select all the text in the text box and change the font to Berlin Sans FB, the font size to 24 points, and the font color to Blue, Accent 5, Darker 50%.

6. Save the document with the name **5-Heart**.
7. Print and then close **5-Heart.docx**.

Assessment 3

Data Files

Create a Flyer That Promotes Island Rentals

1. At a blank document, create a flyer advertising a rental program for island vacation condominiums. (Figure WB-5.3 shows a sample document. Use your own design ideas for the flyer.) Include the following text and specifications:
   a. The name of the rental company is *Beach Time Rentals, Inc.*
   b. Prepare a logo with WordArt and possibly an image.
   c. Insert an appropriate number of beach photographs.
   d. Include the following text, formatting it as shown in Figure WB-5.3:
   Vacation at the celebrated Lowcountry islands of Kiawah and Seabrook near historic Charleston, South Carolina. Beach Time Rentals, Inc. offers a variety of unique condos, villas, and homes on Kiawah and Seabrook. For more information on our short- and long-term rental programs, call 843.555.1150 or 1.800.555.4765. Office hours: 9 a.m. to 5 p.m. Monday through Friday 9 a.m. to 6 p.m. Saturday. Visit us online at emcp.net/beachtime
2. Embed an Excel table of temperatures by completing the following steps:
   a. Open Excel and then open **Temperatures.xlsx** from the C5 folder.
   b. Select cells A1:D16 and then click the Copy button on the Home tab.
   c. Make the Word flyer document active, click the Paste button arrow in the Clipboard group on the Home tab, and then click *Paste Special* at the drop-down list. At the Paste Special dialog box, click *Microsoft Excel Worksheet Object* in the *As* list box, make sure the *Paste* option is selected, and then click OK.
   d. Right-click the temperature table, click *Format AutoShape/Picture*, click the Layout tab at the Format Object dialog box, click *In Front of text* in the *Wrapping style* section, and then click OK.
   e. Position the table as desired.
3. Close Excel.
4. In Word, save the document with the name **5-Rentals**.
5. Print and then close **5-Rentals.docx**.

Figure WB-5.3 Sample Solution for Assessment 3

	High	Low	Water
January	59	38	52
February	61	42	54
March	67	46	59
April	76	55	67
May	82	62	72
June	86	68	82
July	89	71	84
August	89	71	84
September	84	67	80
October	77	57	73
November	68	47	63
December	61	39	54
Average	75	55	69

Visual Benchmark

Create a College Flyer

Data Files

1. At a blank document, create a flyer promoting the spring session of classes at Midwest College in Oak Park, Illinois, as shown in Figure WB-5.4 with the following specifications:
   a. Type SUMMER, 2018, and Midwest in three separate text boxes and arrange them attractively. ***Hint: You may want to layer the design objects and change the text wrapping.***
   b. Include the following text in one text box (applying bullets as shown in the figure):
      Summer is a chance to: Learn new skills. Complete a required course. Take one course at a time. Have time to work while taking a class.
   c. Include the following text in another text box:
      Dates to note: Summer Session, May 28 to July 27
      Call 708.555.0148 or register online at emcp.net/midwest/summer
   d. Include the following text in another text box:
      Midwest College
      567 Main Street, Oak Park, IL 60304-8019 708.555.0148
      (or use the name and address of your college)
   e. Insert **college.png** from the C5 folder and then crop, resize, and position the image as shown.
   f. Apply the Pastels Smooth artistic effect to the image.
   g. Apply the Fill: Orange, Accent color 2; Outline: Orange, Accent color 2 (third column, first row) text effect to the text *Midwest College*.
   h. Make any necessary edits and arrange all the objects similarly to what is shown in the figure.

2. Save the completed document with the name **5-College**.
3. Print and then close **5-College.docx**.

Figure WB-5.4 Flyer Created in Visual Benchmark

Case Study

Part 1

Data Files

You work at Impressions Art Gallery and one of your responsibilities is to create announcements for upcoming art shows. Open **IAGLtrhd.docx** to view the font and colors used in the gallery's letterhead. Using what you learned in this chapter, create an announcement for an art show that includes the following information:

- The featured artist is Mariah Salazar and her artistic style is scenic decorative art.
- The show is scheduled for May 4, 2018, from 3:00 p.m. to 9:00 p.m.
- The show will take place at Impressions Art Gallery, located at 1919 Division Street, Harrisburg, Pennsylvania 10107.
- Add your name as the contact person and include the contact phone number (717) 555-7700.
- Add and format any images or shapes that will enhance the appearance of the announcement.

Save the announcement with the name **5-IAGAnnounce**. Print and then close the announcement.

Part 2

Data Files

The owner of Impressions Art Gallery has asked you to create a flyer that will be available at the front desk. The flyer will provide information for anyone interested in having an art show at the gallery. Open **IAGLtrhd.docx** to view the font and font colors used in the gallery's letterhead. Using text boxes, create a simple flyer that includes the following information:

- The gallery's name, Impressions Art Gallery
- A brief description of what the gallery has to offer for art shows, such as the following text:
  Impressions Art Gallery showcases ambitious, original, bold, and inspiring art created through diverse types of styles and particularly focuses on local artists. We provide a number of dates and times for showcasing a local artist's work. Please contact [your name] at (717) 555-7700 to learn how to contract an art show with Impressions Art Gallery.
- An image or shape formatted to match the colors of the flyer
- Color applied to the text box(es)

Save the flyer with the name **5-IAGFlyer**. Print and then close the flyer.

CHAPTER 6

Creating Newsletters

Study Tools

Study tools include a presentation and a glossary. Use these resources to help you further develop and review skills learned in this chapter.

Concepts Check

Check your understanding by identifying application tools used in this chapter. If you are a SNAP user, launch the Concepts Check from your Assignments page.

Recheck

Check your understanding by taking this quiz. If you are a SNAP user, launch the Recheck from your Assignments page.

Skills Assessment

Assessment 1

Create Original Nameplates

Design and then create two nameplates (including subtitle, folio, graphics, and/or logo) for two newsletters for organizations, schools, or businesses (real or fictional).

1. Prepare thumbnail sketches of your designs. Create one nameplate using an asymmetrical design. Also include an image, WordArt, or special character symbol in at least one of the nameplates.
2. Save the first nameplate document with the name **6-NameplateA**.
3. Print and then close **6-NameplateA.docx**. Attach your thumbnail sketch of this design to the printout.
4. Save the second nameplate document with the name **6-NameplateB**.
5. Print and then close **6-NameplateB.docx**. Attach your thumbnail sketch of this design to the printout.

Assessment 2

Data Files

Identify the Parts of a Newsletter

In this assessment, you will open a newsletter and identify specific elements of it.

1. Open **DownbeatWeekly.docx** from the C6 folder and save it with the name **6-DownbeatWeekly.docx**.
2. Review the newsletter for the elements listed below. Label those elements that you find by inserting text boxes with lines drawn from the text boxes to the elements directly into the newsletter document. (Not all the elements are included in the newsletter.)

caption	jump line	✓spot color
✓ end sign	✓kicker	✓subheads
✓ folio	✓masthead	✓subtitle
✓footer	✓nameplate	✓table of contents
✓header	pull quote	
✓ headlines	sidebar	

3. Save, print, and then close **6-DownbeatWeekly**.

Assessment 3

Data Files

Create a Newsletter for an Optometrist

In this assessment, you will create a newsletter for Naper Grove Vision Care that will be distributed to patients. Figure WB-6.1 is provided as a sample newsletter. Create a newsletter using your own design ideas and knowledge of the newsletter concepts and Word features presented in this chapter. Include the following specifications:

1. Prepare a thumbnail sketch of your design.
2. Create an attention-getting nameplate.
3. Use appropriate fonts and text effects.
4. Insert **FocalPoints.docx** from the C6 folder.
5. Consider using a photo and adding picture effects.
6. ***Optional:*** Include an inspirational, popular, or thought-provoking quotation at the end of the newsletter. Books of popular quotations are available at your public library and school library and on the Internet. (Use a search engine and search for "quotes.")
7. Save your newsletter with the name **6-Eyes**.
8. Save the newsletter as a PDF and name it **6-EyesPDF**.
9. After viewing the newsletter in PDF format, close Adobe Reader.
10. Save, print, and then close **6-Eyes.docx**. Attach your thumbnail sketch.

Assessment 4

Data Files

Complete a Mail Merge in a Newsletter

In this assessment, you will open a Word document and then merge it with a data source file (Access database). You will print two copies of the Naper Grove Vision Care newsletter created in Assessment 3. Then, you will print the first page of the merged document on the back of one copy and the last page of the merged document on the back of the second copy. Figure WB-6.2 shows how the back of the first copy will look when you are finished. To create the merged document and print the necessary pages, complete the following steps:

1. Print two copies of the Naper Grove newsletter, **6-Eyes.docx**. You will print on the backs of these copies in Step 8.
2. Open **NGAddressMain.docx** from the C6 folder and save it with the name **6-NGAddressMain**.
3. Click the Mailings tab, click the Select Recipients button in the Start Mail Merge group, and then click *Use an Existing List* at the drop-down list. At the Select Data Source dialog box, navigate to the C6 folder and then double-click ***NaperGrovePatients.mdb***.
4. Position the insertion point inside the text box that displays right of the clip art image located toward the bottom of the document and then click the Address Block button in the Write & Insert Fields group on the Mailings tab. At the Insert Address Block dialog box, click OK.
5. Remove the shape outline from the address text box.
6. Click the Finish & Merge button in the Finish group on the Mailings tab and then click the *Edit Individual Documents* option at the drop-down list. At the Merge to New Document dialog box, make sure that *All* is selected and then click OK.
7. Save the merged letters with the name **6-NGAddresses**.
8. Print the first merged letter on the back of one copy of **6-Eyes.docx** and the last merged letter on the back of the second copy of that document.
9. Close **6-NGAddresses.docx** and then fold each newsletter with the address displaying on the outside so it is ready to mail.
10. Save and then close **6-NGAddressMain.docx**.

Figure WB-6.1 Sample Solution for Assessment 3

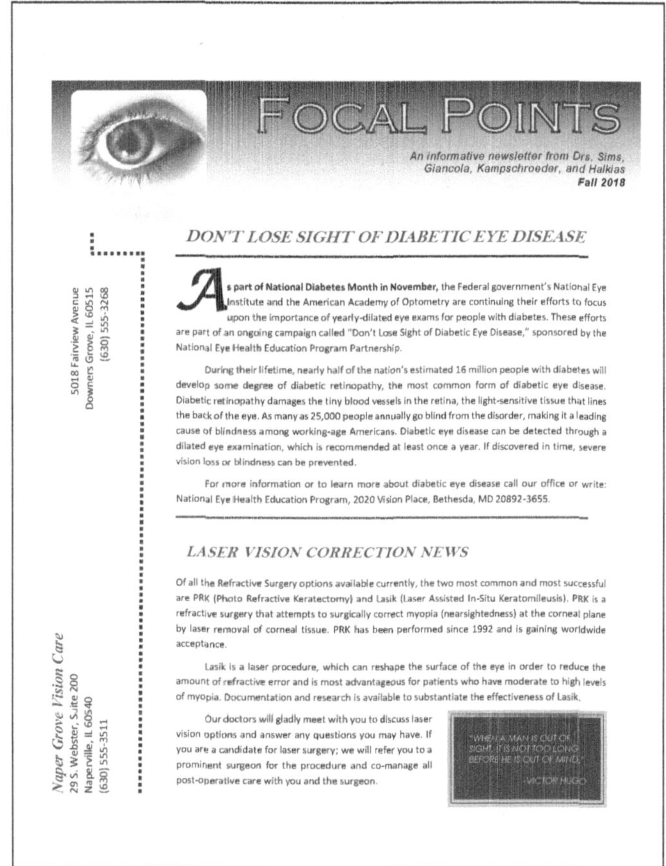

FOCAL POINTS

An informative newsletter from Drs. Sims, Giancola, Kampschroeder, and Halkias
Fall 2018

DON'T LOSE SIGHT OF DIABETIC EYE DISEASE

As part of National Diabetes Month in November, the Federal government's National Eye Institute and the American Academy of Optometry are continuing their efforts to focus upon the importance of yearly-dilated eye exams for people with diabetes. These efforts are part of an ongoing campaign called "Don't Lose Sight of Diabetic Eye Disease," sponsored by the National Eye Health Education Program Partnership.

During their lifetime, nearly half of the nation's estimated 16 million people with diabetes will develop some degree of diabetic retinopathy, the most common form of diabetic eye disease. Diabetic retinopathy damages the tiny blood vessels in the retina, the light-sensitive tissue that lines the back of the eye. As many as 25,000 people annually go blind from the disorder, making it a leading cause of blindness among working-age Americans. Diabetic eye disease can be detected through a dilated eye examination, which is recommended at least once a year. If discovered in time, severe vision loss or blindness can be prevented.

For more information or to learn more about diabetic eye disease call our office or write: National Eye Health Education Program, 2020 Vision Place, Bethesda, MD 20892-3655.

LASER VISION CORRECTION NEWS

Of all the Refractive Surgery options available currently, the two most common and most successful are PRK (Photo Refractive Keratectomy) and Lasik (Laser Assisted In-Situ Keratomileusis). PRK is a refractive surgery that attempts to surgically correct myopia (nearsightedness) at the corneal plane by laser removal of corneal tissue. PRK has been performed since 1992 and is gaining worldwide acceptance.

Lasik is a laser procedure, which can reshape the surface of the eye in order to reduce the amount of refractive error and is most advantageous for patients who have moderate to high levels of myopia. Documentation and research is available to substantiate the effectiveness of Lasik.

Our doctors will gladly meet with you to discuss laser vision options and answer any questions you may have. If you are a candidate for laser surgery; we will refer you to a prominent surgeon for the procedure and co-manage all post-operative care with you and the surgeon.

"WHEN A MAN IS OUT OF SIGHT, IT IS NOT TOO LONG BEFORE HE IS OUT OF MIND."
-VICTOR HUGO

5018 Fairview Avenue
Downers Grove, IL 60515
(630) 555-3268

Naper Grove Vision Care
29 S. Webster, Suite 200
Naperville, IL 60540
(630) 555-3511

Figure WB-6.2 Completed Back of First Copy in Assessment 4

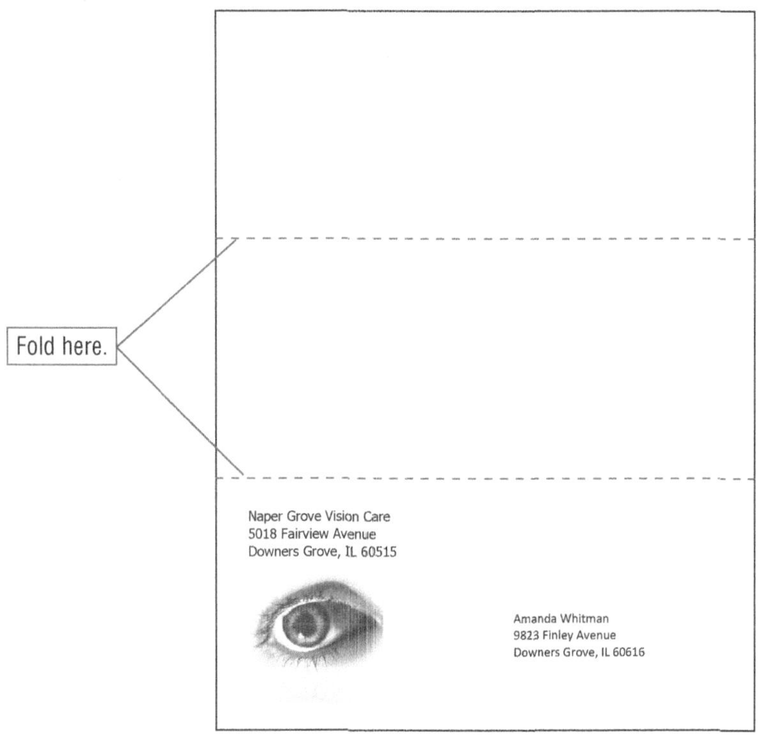

Assessment 5

Data Files

INTEGRATED

Insert an Excel Worksheet as a Visual Aid in a Newsletter

Open **6-SureRideNewsletter.docx**, which you created in Project 2, and then format and embed a worksheet created in Excel on page 2 of the newsletter as shown in Figure WB-6.3. Include the following specifications:

1. Save **6-SureRideNewsletter.docx** with the name **6-SRIntegrated**.
2. Open Excel and at the Excel opening screen, open **SureRideProducts.xlsx**, located in the C6 folder.
3. Enhance the Excel worksheet by completing the following steps:
   a. Select cell A1, which contains *Sure Ride Products – 2018*, click the Fill Color button arrow in the Font group on the Home tab and then click the *Blue, Accent 5* option (ninth column, first row in the *Theme Colors* section).
   b. With cell A1 still selected, click the Borders button arrow in the Font group and then click *More Borders* at the bottom of the drop-down list. At the Format Cells dialog box with the Border tab selected, click the sixth line style in the right column of the *Style* list box, change the *Color* option to Orange (third option in the *Standard Colors* section), click the Outline button in the *Presets* section to add the borders to the preview diagram, and then click OK.
   c. With cell A1 still selected, change the font to 22-point Forte and change the font color to White, Background 1.
   d. Select cells A2:C2, change the font to Impact, and then change the font color to Orange.
   e. Select cells A3:C11 and then change the font to 10-point Franklin Gothic Book.
   f. Select cell A13, click the Format button in the Cells group, click *Row Height* at the drop-down list, type 28, and then click OK.
   g. With cell A13 still selected, change the font to Franklin Gothic Book and then apply italic formatting.
   h. With cell A13 still selected, click the Wrap Text button in the Alignment group.
   i. Select cells C3:C11, click the *Number Format* option box arrow in the Number group, and then click the *Currency* option.
   j. Select cells A1:C13 and then apply the same thick orange border that you applied in Step 3b.
4. Save the Excel worksheet as **6-SureRideProducts**.
5. Select cells A1:C13 and then click the Copy button in the Clipboard group.
6. Minimize Excel and then maximize Word.
7. Delete the last article text within the text box at the bottom of **6-SRIntegrated.docx** (the article *WHEN SHOULD A HELMET BE REPLACED?*).
8. With the insertion point positioned inside the text box, click the Paste button arrow in the Clipboard group on the Home tab and then click *Paste Special* at the drop-down list. Click *Microsoft Excel Worksheet Object* in the Paste Special dialog box and then click OK.
9. If necessary, resize the text box to display the entire Excel object.
10. Save, print, and then close **6-SRIntegrated.docx**.
11. Close **6-SureRideProducts.xlsx** and then close Excel.

Figure WB-6.3 Excel Worksheet Inserted on Page 2 of the Sure Ride Newsletter in Assessment 5

Helmets save lives!

The Light Bulb Test

To illustrate the effectiveness of a bicycle helmet, try the following. Wrap a light bulb in plastic wrap, seal the bottom with a rubber band and place it in a bicycle helmet. Secure the light bulb with tape and drop the helmet onto a flat, hard surface from above your head. The light bulb will not break. In most cases, it will even still light. Now, drop the light bulb without the protection of the helmet. The light bulb will produce a sick thud as it breaks. Helmets *can* make a difference.

Caution: This experiment is meant to be done under close supervision. —●—

▼**ACCIDENTS** *from page 1*

Research indicates that 60% of all U.S. bicycle-car collisions occur among bicyclists between the ages of 8 and 12. Children are permitted to travel with only *"look both ways before you cross the street"* and *"make sure you stop at all stop signs"* warnings. Obviously, these "warnings" are not enough. —●—

Sure Ride

Editor:
Terrence Morrow
Design and Layout:
Sophie Brown
Authors:
Ryan Steele
Sherai McAvoy
Hannan Cantor
Published quarterly by:
Sure Ride, Inc.
P.O. Box 252
Redding, CA 96002
800-555-RIDE
Fax: 530-555-9068

Who Says Helmets Aren't Cool?

Figure 1 Certainly not the children of Shasta, California! One of the biggest reasons children don't wear bicycle helmets is because their friends don't wear them. By getting all the children in your school or neighborhood to order bicycle helmets at the same time, you can help turn this peer pressure from negative to positive. Suddenly, wearing a bicycle helmet becomes the "cool" thing to do. With your support, your kids can be "cool," too!

Sure Ride Products - 2018

Product	Description	Cost
RS1000	Helmet, choice of colors, 3 sizes	$14.99
XSAir	Helmet, Tattoo design, 1 size	$16.99
RS4000	In-Line Skating Helmet, 6 colors, 2 sizes	$22.99
SL100	Flashing Helmet Safety Light	$5.99
SL200	Night Eye Flashing Bicycle Safety Light	$7.99
PG200	In-Line Skating Protective Gear	$32.99
W300	Ride Safe Four Water Bottle	$2.99
S100	Reflective Sweatshirts, 4 sizes	$28.99
T100	Reflective T-Shirts, 5 sizes	$22.99

**All of the Sure Ride bicycle and in-line skating helmets are independently certified to the stringent A.N.S.I. and A.S.T.M standards.*

~2~

Visual Benchmark

Create a Desktop Publishing Training Newsletter

Data Files

1. Open **DTPTraining.docx** and save it with the name **6-DTPTraining**. Format the newsletter so it appears similar to what is shown in Figure WB-6.4 by completing the following steps:
   a. Change the shape fill of the folio to Blue, Accent 5, Darker 25%.
   b. Press Ctrl + End to move the insertion point below the section break, display the Columns dialog box, click the *Left* column option and then change the spacing between columns to 0.4 inch.
   c. Insert a text box for the sidebar as shown in Figure WB-6.4 and then insert the file **MarkCalendar.docx**. If necessary, change the height or width of the text box to display all the text, and then apply the Offset: Bottom Right shadow effect to the text box.
   d. Insert a text box for the table of contents as shown in Figure WB-6.4 and then insert **DesktopTOC.docx** in the text box. Insert a 2 ¼ pt single-line border in Blue, Accent 5, Darker 25% at the top of the text box. If necessary, change the height or width of the text box to display all the text, and then remove the shape outline from the text box.
   e. Insert a text box for the first article as shown in Figure WB-6.4. With the insertion point positioned in the text box, type the kicker (*Two Ways to Learn...*) and then press the Enter key. Insert the file **TrainingTech.docx**. Format the font size and font color of the kicker text and headline text as shown in the figure. Change spacing before or after paragraphs so the article displays as shown in the figure. Remove the shape outline from the text box.
   f. Insert the end sign at the end of the first article using the diamond symbol (Wingdings 2 font and character code 179). Change the color of the end sign to Gold, Accent 4, Darker 25%.
   g. Insert a horizontal line below the first article, as shown in the figure, and then change the shape outline of the line to Blue, Accent 5, Darker 25%. ***Hint: Create a horizontal line by inserting a line shape or adding a bottom border to the text box.***
   h. Insert a text box for the second article shown in Figure WB-6.4. With the insertion point positioned in the text box, type the kicker (*Desktop Resources...*) and then press the Enter key. Insert the file **Knowledge.docx**. Format the font size and font color of the kicker text and headline text as shown in the figure. Change spacing before or after paragraphs so the article displays as shown in the figure. Remove the shape outline from the text box.
   i. Insert and format the jump line at the end of the second article, as shown in the figure.
   j. Insert the image **newsletter.png** and then size and position the image as shown in the figure.
2. Make any necessary changes to the text boxes, text, or graphics so that your newsletter appears similar to what is shown in Figure WB-6.4.
3. Save, print, and then close **6-DTPTraining.docx**.

Figure WB-6.4 Newsletter Created in the Visual Benchmark

From the
DESKTOP

Volume 2 – Issue 3 ***March 2018***

✍Mark Your Calendar:

Workshop:

Desktop Publishing Using Microsoft Word 2016

This workshop will help you learn how your students can meet today's demand for desktop publishing skills on the job using Microsoft Word 2016.

Presenter:
Nancy Stanko
College of DuPage

When:
April 18, 2018
1-4 p.m.

Where:
Okemos Community College
Room 3067
2040 Mount Hope Road
Okemos, MI 47851

Cost:
$50 – includes materials and disk

To reserve your place,
call (800) 555-6018

INSIDE THIS ISSUE

Two Ways to Learn...

Training Techniques

Two types of training are available for those just beginning in desktop publishing.

The first type is a content-based program. This program is based on a typical college program and the information is presented in a classroom situation. Classroom time is usually divided between the presentation of concepts or theory and directed hands-on training. Instructional books and videos are frequently utilized.

Skill-based training is another type of training. This training is useful to businesses because skill-based training produces capable people quickly. Productive skills are put to use on the type of job the person will be expected to fulfill.

Both types of training can produce workers with equal productivity and confidence. The best equipment is wasted if people are not trained to use it efficiently. Good training, regardless of which type, is essential to desktop publishing. ◈

Desktop Resources...

Knowledge Is Power

How can one have up-to-date knowledge needed to keep on the cutting edge of desktop publishing? One way to gain desktop publishing knowledge is to read, read, read! Read some of the periodicals, newsletters, and books now available that address all aspects of desktop publishing.

Two basic types of periodicals are available. The first type is based on technological development and communication arts. These periodicals contain useful information about current and new products. The second type contains knowledge of technique, style, and applications.

Many newsletters and books are available. Your local library and bookstores can be good sources for resource material.

(See *Knowledge Is Power* on page 2)

From the Desktop 1

Case Study

Part
1

Data Files

You work for Butterfield Gardens, which is a local nursery and landscaping business. Your supervisor has asked you to evaluate the current newsletter and then re-create it. Open **ButterfieldGardens.docx** and then save it with the name **6-Butterfield**. The newsletter looks relatively neat and organized, but with closer inspection, you notice a few errors in spelling, formatting, layout, and design. Re-create the newsletter according to the following specifications, using your own ideas for an interesting newsletter layout and design:

- Prepare a thumbnail sketch of your design.
- Re-create the nameplate or create a nameplate (newsletter title, company logo) of your own for this company; consider using WordArt in your nameplate design. ***Hint: The Butterfield Gardens logo is located in the C6 folder.***
- Create a different layout and design for the newsletter using columns. Use more than one column in an asymmetrical design or consider using an online template.
- Correct all the spelling and formatting errors. ***Hint: The document contains several errors.***
- Use any images that support your design. Consider using a drawing or photo from the Internet.
- Consider inserting a shape or chart.
- Use any newsletter elements and enhancements that will improve the effectiveness and appeal of this newsletter. ***Hint: Remember to kern character pairs and condense or expand characters if necessary.***

Save and then print **6-Butterfield.docx**. Attach the thumbnail sketch to the back of the newsletter.

Part
2

Your supervisor liked the design of the newsletter you created for Butterfield Gardens and has asked you to add content to it. Search the Internet and find interesting articles about gardening to include on the second page of the newsletter. Type gardening in the search text box at www.google.com, www.bing.com, or any search engine of your choosing. With **6-Butterfield.docx** open, save it with the name **6-BGNewsletter**. Insert the additional information you found on the Internet. Make sure to create bylines to give credit to the authors of the articles you have used. Search for and select images that reinforce the message. Keep in mind the topic of the newsletter and the intended audience. Save and then print **6-BGNewsletter.docx**.

Part
3

The Butterfield Gardens newsletter will be sent electronically as an attachment to an email, so your supervisor has asked you to create a PDF of the revised newsletter. With **6-BGNewsletter.docx** open, create a PDF version of the newsletter and name it **6-BGNewsletterPDF**.

Part
4

Data Files

Open **DocumentEvaluationChecklist.docx** and then save it with the name **6-Evaluation**. Open **6-BGNewsletter.docx** and then evaluate your revised newsletter using the checklist. Save, print, and then close **6-Evaluation.docx**.

Creating Brochures and Booklets

CHAPTER 7

Study Tools

Study tools include a presentation and a glossary. Use these resources to help you further develop and review skills learned in this chapter.

Concepts Check

Check your understanding by identifying application tools used in this chapter. If you are a SNAP user, launch the Concepts Check from your Assignments page.

Recheck

Check your understanding by taking this quiz. If you are a SNAP user, launch the Recheck from your Assignments page.

Skills Assessment

Assessment

1

Data Files

Create Inside Panels for a Letter-fold Brochure

As a supportive member of the Newport Volunteer Center, you have volunteered to use your desktop publishing skills to create a promotional brochure for the center. Your target audience includes the general public, but more specifically, it includes volunteers, organizations in need of volunteers, and community organizers. Your audience will mainly consist of adults but keep children in mind. Your purpose is to let your readers know what the volunteer center has to offer. The content of your brochure will include information on volunteer opportunities, volunteer programs, scheduled events, and contact information.

In this first assessment, you will create panels 1, 2, and 3 (the inside panels) of the Newport Volunteer Center brochure. In Assessment 2, you will create panels 4, 5, and 6 (the outside panels) of the brochure. An example of a complete brochure is provided in Figures WB-7.1 on page WB-64 (front) and WB-7.2 on page WB-65 (back); however, you are to create your own design (using text from the C7 folder). Complete your brochure according to the following specifications:

1. Create a letter-fold brochure. You can create the brochure layout from scratch using text boxes, columns, or tables. Alternatively, you can use one of the brochure templates at Office.com or any other template source.
2. Include all the information contained in **VolunteerText.docx** in the C7 folder.
3. Create a thumbnail sketch of your design and then create a dummy to guide you in the placement of text.
4. Select an appropriate theme and then apply, create, and/or modify styles.
5. Use relevant graphics. A large selection of volunteer-related images can be viewed by displaying the Insert Pictures window and searching for images using the keywords *volunteer* and *community*. Viewing these images may help to inspire the design and the color scheme of your brochure. Photographs tend to support a sophisticated design.

6. Use a coordinated color scheme. Remember that you can customize the text colors to match the color(s) in an image, customize the color(s) of an image to match a specific text color, or coordinate colors within another image.
7. Use appropriate typefaces. Make sure that all the text is legible. Turn on kerning for fonts over 14 points.
8. Make any necessary adjustments to the spacing before and after paragraphs.
9. As you work, evaluate your design for the concepts of focus, balance, proportion, contrast, directional flow, consistency, and color.
10. Save the document containing the inside panels of the brochure in the C7 folder with the name **7-NVCPanels1-3**.
11. Print **7-NVCPanels1-3.docx**.

Figure WB-7.1 Sample Solution for Assessment 1 (Panels 1, 2, and 3 of a Letter-fold Brochure)

WHAT WE DO...

The Newport Volunteer Center provides prospective volunteers opportunities to serve the community. A wide range of opportunities are available for both individuals and groups. Volunteer opportunities can be an ongoing service or a one-time project. The Newport Volunteer Center also provides a platform for local organizations to recruit volunteers or services.

FIND AN OPPORTUNITY

There are many ways to find a volunteer opportunity, including searching our online database, walking into the center, or calling the center. If you have a cause that is important to you, or a particular set of skills you want to use, the Newport Volunteer Center can provide you with an opportunity that fits you best.

VOLUNTEER OPPORTUNITIES ARE LIMITLESS...

- Clean up a park
- Build a home
- Raise funds for an organization
- Work at an animal shelter
- Organize, coordinate and host an event
- Mentor a child
- Visit with senior citizens
- Provide consulting services
- Provide translation services
- Many more activities

SCHEDULED EVENTS

In addition to finding an opportunity that suits you, the Newport Volunteer Center also hosts a number of service events. The following events are county-wide, annual events on which you can serve:

- Martin Luther King, Jr. Day of Service, *third Monday in January*
- Earth Day, *April 22*
- Community Service Day, *fourth Saturday in October*
- Veteran's Day, *November 11*
- Thanksgiving, *fourth Thursday in November*
- Secret Santa, *December 1 to December 24*

YOUTH VOLUNTEER PROGRAM

The Youth Volunteer program provides young people, ages 10 and older, with appropriate volunteer opportunities that will help them learn new skills and earn community service hours.

RSVP: RETIRED AND SENIOR VOLUNTEER PROGRAM

The Retired and Senior Volunteer Program (RSVP) provides seniors, age 55 and older, with appropriate volunteer opportunities that will utilize the current skill set of the volunteer. RSVP volunteers get added benefits, such as insurance while volunteering.

Assessment 2

Data Files

Create Outside Panels for a Letter-fold Brochure

In this assessment, you will create panels 4, 5, and 6 of the Newport Volunteer Center brochure that you started in Assessment 1. Include the following specifications:

1. With **7-NVCPanels1-3.docx** open, save the document with the name **7-NVCBrochure**.
2. Refer to the dummy you created in Assessment 1 to create the outside panels of the brochure. A sample solution is provided in Figure WB-7.2.
3. Apply any relevant styles according to the design you established in Assessment 1.
4. Make any necessary adjustments to the spacing and positioning of text.
5. After creating and modifying styles, save the style set as **XX-NVCStyles** (replacing the *XX* with your initials).
6. Save **7-NVCBrochure.docx**.
7. Print panels 4, 5, and 6 on the back side of the **7-NVCPanels1-3.docx** brochure that you printed in Assessment 1. Fold the brochure and check the placement of the text and images in relation to the folds. Make adjustments as necessary to produce a professional-looking finished brochure.
8. Open **DocumentEvaluationChecklist.docx** in the C7 folder and then save the document with the name **7-Analysis-2**. Use the checklist to evaluate your brochure design. Save, print, and then close **7-Analysis-2.docx**.
9. Close **7-NVCBrochure.docx**.

Figure WB-7.2 Sample Solution for Assessment 2 (Panels 4, 5, and 6 of a Letter-fold Brochure)

CONSULTANT PROGRAM

Use your professional skills in a meaningful and challenging way while giving back to the community. Consultants help nonprofits and government agencies with projects in various fields such as accounting, website design, marketing, writing, planning and research.

COMMUNITY ORGANIZATIONS AND GROUPS

The Newport Volunteer Center helps local organizations and groups build relationships with nonprofits and government agencies. The Newport Volunteer Center works to connect community organizations and groups with other organizations or groups needing assistance. Search for group volunteer opportunities on the online database.

COURT REFERRAL PROGRAM

The Newport Volunteer Center works with local government agencies to assist individuals who are required to complete community service work. The Newport Volunteer Center provides placement, follow-up, and monitoring of adult and juvenile offenders. Find out more about the Court Referral Program at the website.

STAY CONNECTED

Keep up to date with the most recent volunteer opportunities, volunteering trends, and volunteer events.

VISIT OUR WEBSITE

www.emcp.net/nvc

SUBSCRIBE TO NEWPORT VOLUNTEER

Our monthly newsletter

CALL

(584) 555-1212

EMAIL

newportvc@emcp.net

NEWPORT VOLUNTEER CENTER

HOW WILL YOU SERVE?

NEWPORT VOLUNTEER CENTER

Assessment 3

Data Files

Create a Brochure for Mailing

Adapting the design style and content that you used in Assessments 1 and 2, use the 2 Pages per Sheet feature to create a brochure that will be mailed out to the local community. A sample brochure is provided in Figure WB-7.3. Your brochure should not match this sample but should instead be similar to your Assessment 1 and 2 documents in terms of design and style. Include the following specifications in your design:

1. Starting at a blank document, modify the page setup to create a 2 pages per sheet page layout.
2. If you created a custom style set in Assessment 2, use it to keep the design and formatting consistent between the brochures.
3. Create the inside panels before creating the outside panels.
4. Choose the text to include in the brochure from the **VolunteerText.docx** file in the C7 folder.
5. Use the sample solution shown in Figure WB-7.3 for ideas on the layout of the brochure. However, create your own design using elements from the brochures created in the previous assessments.
6. Use shapes, text boxes, clip art, SmartArt, and other types of desktop publishing elements to enhance the appearance of the document. Reuse elements that you used in Assessments 1 and 2 to maintain a consistent appearance among the brochures.
7. Create a self-mailer by typing the following return address on the back cover of the brochure:

   Newport Volunteer Center
   2647 Saldago Drive East
   Newport, OR 97366
8. Save the document with the name **7-NVCMailer**.
9. Print the first page of the brochure and then print the second page on the back of the first page. Fold the brochure and then check the placement of text and images in relation to the folds. Make any adjustments necessary to produce a professional and polished final brochure.
10. Close **7-NVCMailer.docx**.

Figure WB-7.3 Sample Solution for Assessment 3 (2 Pages per Sheet Layout)

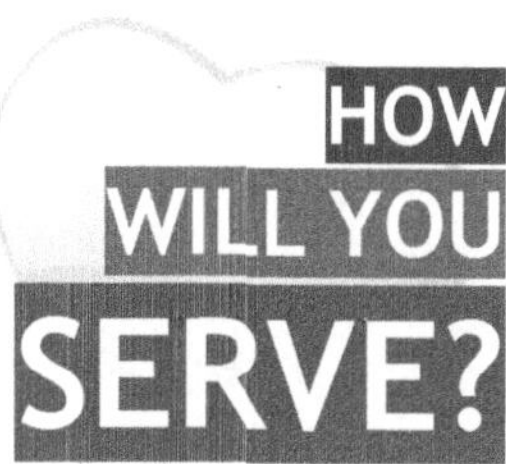

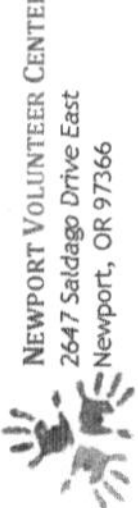

WHAT WE DO...

The Newport Volunteer Center provides prospective volunteers opportunities to serve the community. A wide range of opportunities are available for both individuals and groups. Volunteer opportunities can be an ongoing service or a one-time project. The Newport Volunteer Center also provides a platform for local organizations to recruit volunteers or services.

FIND AN OPPORTUNITY

There are many ways to find a volunteer opportunity, including searching our online database, walking into the center, or calling the center. If you have a cause that is important to you, or a particular set of skills you want to use, the Newport Volunteer Center can provide you with an opportunity that fits you best.

VOLUNTEER OPPORTUNITIES ARE LIMITLESS...

- Clean up a park
- Build a home
- Raise funds for an organization
- Work at an animal shelter
- Organize, coordinate and host an event
- Mentor a child
- Visit with senior citizens
- Provide consulting services
- Provide translation services

SCHEDULED EVENTS

In addition to finding an opportunity that suits you, the Newport Volunteer Center also hosts a number of service events. The following events are county-wide, annual events on which you can serve:

- Martin Luther King, Jr. Day of Service, *third Monday in January*
- Earth Day, *April 22*
- Community Service Day, *fourth Saturday in October*
- Veteran's Day, *November 11*
- Thanksgiving, *fourth Thursday in November*
- Secret Santa, *December 1 to December 24*

YOUTH VOLUNTEER PROGRAM

The Youth Volunteer program provides young people, ages 10 and older, with appropriate volunteer opportunities that will help them learn new skills and earn community service hours.

RSVP: RETIRED AND SENIOR VOLUNTEER PROGRAM

The Retired and Senior Volunteer Program (RSVP) provides seniors, age 55 and older, with appropriate volunteer opportunities that will utilize the current skill set of the volunteer. RSVP volunteers get added benefits such as insurance while volunteering.

COURT REFERRAL PROGRAM

The Newport Volunteer Center works with local government agencies to assist individuals who are required to complete community service work. The Newport Volunteer Center provides placement, follow-up, and monitoring of adult and juvenile offenders. Find out more about the Court Referral Program at the website.

STAY CONNECTED

Keep up to date with the most recent volunteer opportunities, volunteering trends, and volunteer events.

VISIT OUR WEBSITE

www.emcp.net/nvc

SUBSCRIBE TO NEWPORT VOLUNTEER

Our monthly newsletter

CALL

(584) 555-1212

EMAIL

newportvc@emcp.net

Assessment 4

Data Files

GROUP PROJECT

INTEGRATED

Create a Fundraising Brochure Containing a Chart

You are a member of the fund-raising committee for Summit Outreach Community Services. With the help of the other members of your group, plan an event to raise money and create a brochure that promotes the charity and advertises the event. A sample solution is shown in Figure WB-7.4. Your brochure may use similar elements and content but should not look exactly like the sample. Include the following specifications in your design:

1. Use the **SOLogo.png**, **SOLogo+Text.png**, and **bag.png** images from the C7 folder.
2. Include a chart that illustrates the increase in the number of families served over the past three years. An example is shown in Figure WB-7.4. Use Excel to create the chart or use Word to create a column chart, as shown in the sample solution. In the sample solution, **bag.png** was used as a fill for the data columns in the graph.
3. Use the text in the sample document, or if it is difficult to read, open **SOText.docx** from the C7 folder. Another option is to research a similar organization and fund-raising event on the Internet for facts, information, goals, and so on and then write the text yourself.
4. Save the completed brochure with the name **7-Fundraiser.docx**.
5. Print the brochure.
6. Open **DocumentEvaluationChecklist.docx** in the C7 folder and then save it with the name **7-Analysis-4**.
7. Use the document evaluation checklist to analyze your brochure and make additional adjustments, if necessary.
8. Save, print, and then close **7-Analysis-4.docx**.
9. Close **7-Fundraiser.docx**.
10. Staple the completed document evaluation to the back of your brochure.

Figure WB-7.4 Sample Solution for Assessment 4

Our Needs Have Increased

SUMMIT
OUTREACH

- 1,676 families (5,766 individuals)
- 160 seniors and disabled individuals
- 2,080 children, from infants to 18-year-olds

Number of Families Has Increased 63% Since 2016

1200
1000
800
600
400
200
0

701 959 1140

2016 2017 2018

How You Can Help

Cash donations are especially welcome. Your dollars go farther when we do the shopping. Any other food is welcome!

Help us help others this holiday season!

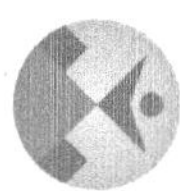

Summit Outreach Community Services
884 Alder Lane
Bellingham, WA 98225

Please join us for our first annual

Help us feed Bellingham's hungry

Did You Know?

- There are over 4,000 individuals in Bellingham living in poverty.
- A 2-bedroom apartment in Bellingham costs a minimum of **$900/month.**
- A minimum wage-earner makes approximately **$1200/month** (gross) working a 40-hour week.
- This leaves less than **$300/month** for food, clothing, and utilities.

Summit Outreach:

- Distributes in excess of 770,000 pounds of food to families in need, annually.
- Has had a **250%** increase of families served over the last five years.
- Has provided food and personal care essentials to Bellingham residents in need for **23 years.**
- Is community-run, operated by volunteers and supported by donations from the Bellingham community at large.

When

Sunday, December 16, 2018

Open House, 6:30 p.m. to 10:00 p.m.

Where

Summit Outreach Community Services
884 Alder Lane
Bellingham, WA 98225

Tickets

$50 per ticket ($30 tax deductible)

Events

- Cocktails
- Picnic, hot and cold hors d'oeuvres
- Silent auction
- Music and entertainment

Please respond by Monday, November 26

☐ I/we request ______________ reservations at $50 per person ($30 tax deductible).

☐ I am unable to attend, but please accept my monetary donation to the food pantry.

☐ Enclosed is my check for $ ________ made payable to Loaves & Fishes.

☐ Please charge $ ___________ to my credit card.

☐ Visa ☐ Mastercard ☐ Discover

Name: ____________________

Card number: ________________

Expiration date: ______________

Please use the enclosed envelope to mail your **RSVP** and payment by **Monday, November 26.**

You may also reply by telephone at (360) 555-8110 or send email to **summit@emcp.net**

Visual Benchmark

Format a Brochure for Mailing

Data Files

1. Open **SummitMailer.docx** and then save it with the name **7-SummitMailer**.
2. Copy the Heading 2, Heading 3, and Heading 4 styles from the **SummitTemplate.dotx** template into the current document.
3. Format the document so it appears as shown in Figure WB-7.5 with the following specifications:
   a. Apply the imported styles to the appropriate text.
   b. Create a new style named XX-SummitBody with 11-point Franklin Gothic Book, 6 points of space before paragraphs, and 18 points of space after paragraphs.
   c. Apply the XX-SummitBody style to the body text in the brochure (not the bulleted text).
   d. Rotate, position, and align the address, images, and logos.
   e. Apply picture formatting (such as recoloring and corrections) to the images on the cover.
   f. Apply bulleted list formatting to the text as shown in Figure WB-7.5. ***Note: Use options at the Paragraph dialog box to adjust the spacing of the bulleted items.***
   g. Use **SOLogo.png** as the bullet in the first bulleted list, and use the blank calendar symbol in the Webdings font as the bullet in the second bulleted list.
   h. Insert continuous breaks and apply column formatting to the specific sections.
   i. Perform any further formatting so the brochure appears as shown in Figure WB-7.5.
4. Save, print, and then close **7-SummitMailer.docx**.

Figure WB-7.5 Visual Benchmark

Community Connections...

Summit **Outreach** Community Services
884 Alder Lane
Bellingham, WA 98225

Our Mission...

Summit Outreach provides resource referrals and leadership in the community by coordinating and uniting resources to empower people to be self-sufficient.

Community Connections

Community is what connects our city in ways that inspire, nurture, and support others. On top of the traditional means of fundraising, Summit Outreach depends on the community by receiving food from local markets and farms.

Support the community by...

- Donating Money (tax deductible!)
- Donating Food
- Raising funds for Summit Outreach
- Volunteering at a partner kitchen
- Organizing, coordinating, and hosting an event
- Providing transportation services

Scheduled Events

Summit Outreach hosts a number of events annually in order to provide families with food during important times. The following are currently the annual events that Summit Outreach Community Services hosts:

- Spring Food Faire, *third Saturday in March*
- Memorial Day Barbeque, *last Monday in May*
- Support Our Veterans, *November 11*
- Thanksgiving Drive, *November 12 to fourth Thursday in November*
- Picnic in December, *third Sunday in December*

Need Food? We Can Help!

Summit Outreach is determined to stop families from going hungry. Contact us if you are in need of food or other assistance. We are here to provide those in need with the resources they require to live a healthy life.

Client Choice Program

The Client Choice system allows Summit patrons to select foods they enjoy and know how to prepare, drastically reducing waste. This reduction in waste enables Summit Outreach to provide more food at less cost. Additionally, patrons with health issues will now be able to choose foods that will help, not hurt their medical conditions.

Picnic in December

When:	Where:	Tickets:
December 16, 2018 6:30 p.m. to 10:00 p.m.	884 Alder Lane Bellingham, WA 98225	$50 per ticket ($30 tax deductible)

Stay Connected

Keep up to date with the most recent opportunities, trends, and events at Summit Outreach with the information below.

Find Us!

Call	Email
(360) 555-8110	summit@emcp.net

Case Study

Part 1

Data Files

As Paul Brewster's assistant at a medium-sized flight school, you have been given the task of preparing booklets and brochures that will be mailed to existing and potential customers. Mr. Brewster has created **NWAText.docx**, which includes company information and graphics. Begin by choosing the framework for a brochure, such as a table, columns, or text boxes. At a blank document, begin creating a brochure that contains three panels on each side of the page using one of the folds described in Chapter 7. Create the inside panels by copying and pasting text and images from **NWAText.docx**. Use any Word 2016 features you have learned in this book to enhance the design of the inside panels of the brochure and then save it with the name **7-NWAPanels1-3**. Print **7-NWAPanels1-3.docx**.

Part 2

Data Files

With **7-NWAPanels1-3.docx** open, continue developing the brochure for Mr. Brewster by creating the three outside panels. Copy and paste text and images from **NWAText.docx**, and use any Word 2016 features you have learned in this book to enhance the design of the brochure. Save the brochure with the name **7-NWABrochure1**. Save any styles created or modified for the brochure and then save the brochure as a template with the name 7-**NWATemplate.dotx**. Insert into the printer the page containing the first three panels printed in Part 1 of the Case Study, and then print the last three panels to complete the brochure. Close **7-NWABrochure1.docx**.

Part 3

Using the design elements, graphics, and information from the brochures you created for Mr. Brewster in Parts 1 and 2, create another brochure using the 2 Pages per Sheet feature. Begin by developing the cover and the back panels. Import the styles you created or modified and then saved in the template **7-NWATemplate.dotx**. Save the document with the name **7-NWACoverBack**. Print **7-NWACoverBack.docx**.

Part 4

With **7-NWACoverBack.docx** open, continue developing the second brochure you created for Mr. Brewster by completing the inside panels. Use the design elements, graphics, styles, and text from the brochures you created in Parts 1, 2, and 3. Save the document with the name **7-NWABrochure2**. Print the inside panels on the other side of the page printed in Part 3 and then close **7-NWABrochure2.docx**.

CHAPTER 8

Creating Specialty Promotional Documents

Study Tools

Study tools include a presentation and a glossary. Use these resources to help you further develop and review skills learned in this chapter.

Concepts Check

Check your understanding by identifying application tools used in this chapter. If you are a SNAP user, launch the Concepts Check from your Assignments page.

Recheck

Check your understanding by taking this quiz. If you are a SNAP user, launch the Recheck from your Assignments page.

Skills Assessment

Assessment 1

Data Files

Create a Promotional Gift Certificate

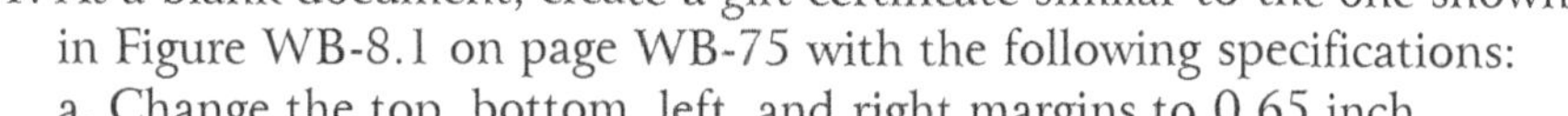

1. At a blank document, create a gift certificate similar to the one shown in Figure WB-8.1 on page WB-75 with the following specifications:
   a. Change the top, bottom, left, and right margins to 0.65 inch.
   b. Create a table with two columns and one row.
   c. Change the row height to 2.65 inches, the width of the first column to 4.75 inches, and the width of the second column to 2.25 inches.
   d. Change the top, left, bottom, and right default cell margins to 0.1 inch. ***Hint: Use the Cell Margins button in the Alignment group on the Table Tools Layout tab.***
   e. Display the Borders and Shading dialog box, click the middle column border in the *Preview* section to remove the border, and then click OK.
   f. Center the table horizontally on the page.
   g. With the insertion point positioned in the first cell, type Gift Certificate and then press the Enter key two times.
   h. Select *Gift Certificate*, change the font to 36-point French Script MT, and then apply the Blue, Accent 5, Darker 25% font color (ninth column, fifth row in the *Theme Colors* section).
   i. Position the insertion point on the blank line below *Gift Certificate* and then set left tabs at 0.5 inch, 1.75 inches, 2.75 inches, and 4.3 inches.
   j. Using the tabs set in the previous step, type the text in the first cell as shown in Figure WB-8.1. To create the underlines, press the spacebar once after typing a text label, click the Underline button on the Home tab, press the spacebar again, and then press Ctrl + Tab to move to the next tab and create the underline. (You may need to press Ctrl + Tab more than once to create an underline of the correct length.) Once you have typed an underline, turn off the underline feature, press the Enter key two times, and then type the next text label. Continue in this manner until you have typed all the text and underlines in the first cell.
   k. Type the text in the second cell as shown in Figure WB-8.1. Center the text and set *Butterfield Gardens* in 24-point French Script MT in the Blue, Accent 5, Darker 25% font color. Remove the hyperlink from the web address if necessary.

2. Insert the Butterfield Gardens logo (**BGLogo.png**) from the C8 folder. Change the color of the logo to Blue, Accent color 5 Light, change the text wrapping to Tight, and then resize and position the logo as shown in Figure WB-8.1.
3. Create two more certificates on the same page by copying and pasting the table. ***Hint: Insert one hard return after each certificate.***
4. Save the document with the name **8-Certificate**.
5. Print and then close **8-Certificate.docx**.

Assessment 2

Data Files

Create and Merge Name Tags

1. At a blank document, create the name tag main document shown in Figure WB-8.2 on page WB-76. Begin by clicking the Mailings tab, clicking the Start Mail Merge button, and then clicking *Labels* at the drop-down list.
2. At the Label Options dialog box, select *Avery US Letter* in the *Label vendors* option box, select *5393 Hanging Name Badges* in the *Product number* list box, and then click OK to close the dialog box.
3. Select the data source file by clicking the Select Recipients button and then clicking *Use an Existing List* at the drop-down list. At the Select Data Source dialog box, navigate to the C8 folder and then double-click ***FloralDataSource.mdb***.
4. With the insertion point positioned inside the first name tag, make the following changes:
   a. Change the spacing before paragraphs to 0 points.
   b. Press the spacebar once, press the Enter key, and then change the font to 11-point Arial Black.
   c. Type the text and insert the field codes in the cell as shown in Figure WB-8.2. Insert the field codes by clicking the Insert Merge Field button arrow on the Mailings tab and then clicking the desired field code at the drop-down list.
   d. Select the fields *«FirstName»*, *«LastName»*, and *«JobTitle»* and then change the font size to 14 points.
   e. Select from the blank line above the fields *«FirstName»* and *«LastName»* through the blank line below *«JobTitle»* and then apply Dark Blue shading (second option from the right in the *Standard Colors* section).
   f. Align the lines of text as shown in Figure WB-8.2.
   g. Click the Update Labels button in the Write & Insert Field group on the Mailings tab.
5. Merge the main document with the data source by clicking the Finish & Merge button, clicking *Edit Individual Documents* at the drop-down list, making sure that *All* is selected in the Merge to New Document dialog box, and then clicking OK.
6. Save the merged document with the name **8-NameTags**.
7. Print and then close **8-NameTags.docx**. (These name tags are designed to be inserted into holders, which are clear plastic sleeves with clips or pins on the reverse sides. Holders are usually available through mail order paper companies and office supply companies.)
8. Save the name tags main document with the name **8-NameTagsMainDoc**.
9. Close **8-NameTagsMainDoc.docx**.

Figure WB-8.1 Gift Certificates Created in Assessment 1

Gift Certificate

Date ______________________

This certificate entitles ______________________

To ______________________ Dollars $ __________

Presented by ______________________

Authorized signature ______________________

Butterfield Gardens
29 W 036 Butterfield Road
Warrenville, IL 60555
(630) 555-1062

www.emcp.net/butterfield

Butterfield GARDENS

Gift Certificate

Date ______________________

This certificate entitles ______________________

To ______________________ Dollars $ __________

Presented by ______________________

Authorized signature ______________________

Butterfield Gardens
29 W 036 Butterfield Road
Warrenville, IL 60555
(630) 555-1062

www.emcp.net/butterfield

Butterfield GARDENS

Gift Certificate

Date ______________________

This certificate entitles ______________________

To ______________________ Dollars $ __________

Presented by ______________________

Authorized signature ______________________

Butterfield Gardens
29 W 036 Butterfield Road
Warrenville, IL 60555
(630) 555-1062

www.emcp.net/butterfield

Butterfield GARDENS

Figure WB-8.2 Name Tag Main Document and Merged Document Created in Assessment 2

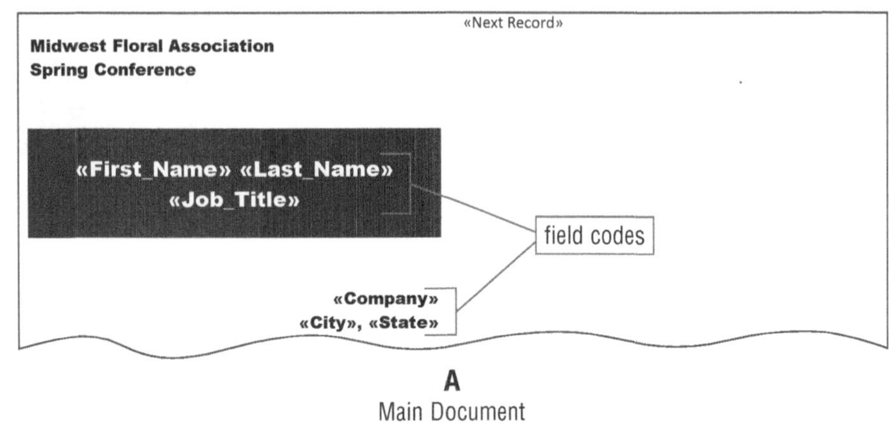

A
Main Document

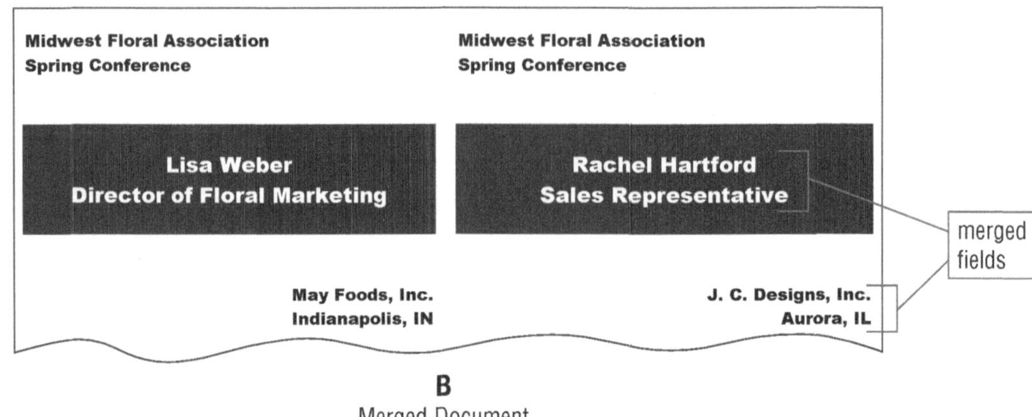

B
Merged Document

Assessment 3

Data Files

Create an Event Invitation

1. At a blank document, create the front panels of the invitation shown in Figure WB-8.3A on page WB-78 with the following specifications:
   a. Change the orientation to landscape and then apply *Narrow* margins.
   b. Insert a table with two columns and two rows and then select the entire table and change the row height to 3.6 inches.
   c. Insert the shading fill color in the bottom two cells using the following custom color: Red = 51, Green = 51, and Blue = 153. ***Hint: Use options at the Colors dialog box with the Custom tab selected to apply the custom color.***
   d. Insert a text box, type the text An evening out on the town!, position the text box in the location indicated in the figure, and then change the font to 16-point Harrington, apply bold formatting, and change the font color to Gold, Accent 4, Lighter 60%.
   e. Position the insertion point at the beginning of the cell containing the text you just typed and then insert **conductor.png** from the C8 folder. Change the text wrapping for the image to In Front of Text and then position the image as shown in Figure WB-8.3A.
   f. Insert **stars1.png** from the C8 folder. Use the Set Transparent Color tool (located in the Color button drop-down gallery in the Adjust group on the Picture Tools Format tab) to remove the white background fill from the image. Change the text wrapping to In Front of Text, change the width of the image to 2.5 inches, and then position the image as shown in Figure WB-8.3A.

g. Copy the images and the text from the first cell in the bottom row to the second cell in the bottom row. Make any adjustments necessary so the text and images in the second cell match the text and images in the first cell.

2. Save the document with the name **8-InvitationCover**.
3. Print and then close **8-InvitationCover.docx**.
4. At a blank document, create the inside panels of the invitation shown in Figure WB-8.3B with the following specifications:
   a. Change the orientation to landscape and then apply *Narrow* margins.
   b. Insert a table with two columns and two rows and then select the entire table and change the row height to 3.6 inches.
   c. Type the text in the first cell in the bottom row as shown in Figure WB-8.3B with the following specifications:
      1) Set the first four lines of text in 14-point Candara and the last two lines of text in 12-point Candara.
      2) Insert the five lines of text starting with *Trattoria 8* inside a text box and set the text in 13-point Candara. Remove the text box shape outline, change the text wrapping to Tight, and position the text box as shown in Figure WB-8.3B.
      3) Insert the five lines of text starting with *Chicago Theater* inside a text box with the same formatting as the first text box.
      4) Apply bold formatting, italic formatting, and center alignment to the text as shown in Figure WB-8.3B.
      5) Apply the Gradient Fill: Gold, Accent color 4; Outline: Gold, Accent color 4 text effect to the text *Evening out on the town* and increase the font size to 18 points.
   d. Insert and position the images **stars2.png** and **stars3.png** from the C8 folder as shown in Figure WB-8.3B.
   e. Copy the text, text boxes, and images from the first cell in the bottom row to the second cell in the bottom row. Make any adjustments necessary so the text, text boxes, and images in the second cell match the text, text boxes, and images in the first cell. ***Hint: Select all of the items before copying them to the second cell, or group the items first and then copy the group to the second cell.***
5. Save the document with the name **8-InvitationInside**.
6. Print **8-InvitationInside.docx** on the back side of **8-InvitationCover.docx** and then close the document.

Assessment 4

Data Files

Design and Create a Promotional Document

1. Form groups of three or four students. Assign necessary group tasks to create a promotional document of your own design based on a sample document you have found or a template located on the Internet. Use any of the Word features you have learned so far. If you are using a sample document, first evaluate the document for good layout and design, a clear and concise message, and proper use of other desktop publishing concepts, as outlined in the Document Analysis Guide (refer to **DocumentAnalysisGuide.docx** in the C8 folder). Some possible promotional documents include the following:
   - Invitation to a new store opening
   - Introduction of a new course at your local community college
   - Invitation to a class reunion
   - Business greeting card or company party invitation

Figure WB-8.3 Invitation Created in Assessment 3

A
Invitation Cover

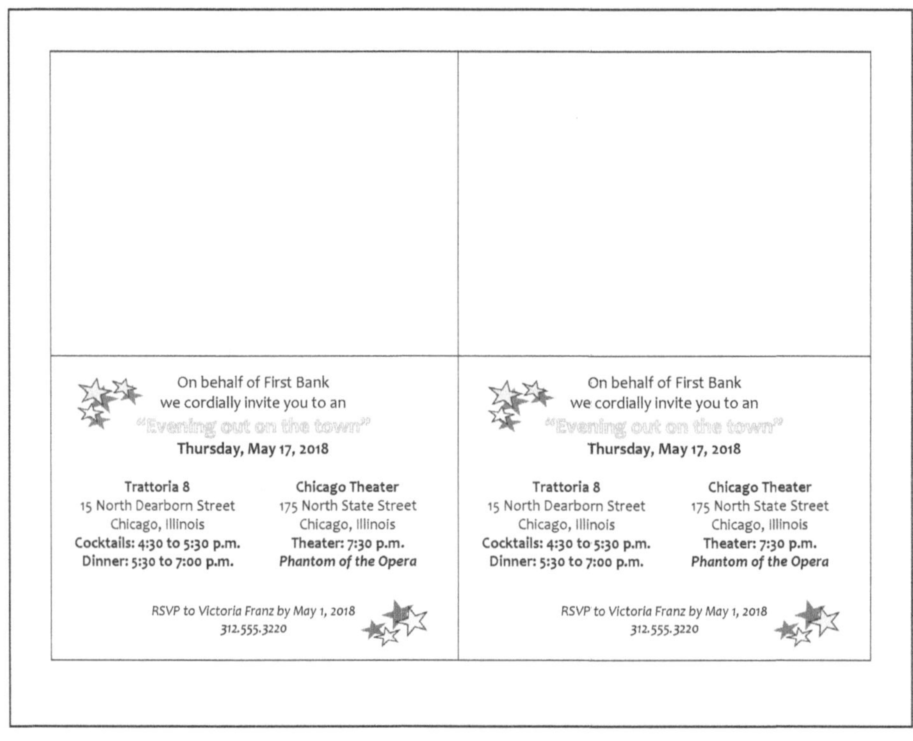

B
Invitation Inside Text

- Postcard as a follow-up or one promoting a new business (coffee shop, party planner, attorney's office, computer service, or health spa as shown in Figure WB-8.4)
- Membership card
- Ticket with a company or organization name or logo
- Form requesting information for membership
- Document used by a service company promoting e-Bill (which allows paying your account balance online)
- Postcard advertising a sample sale
- Poster advertising services at a travel agency

2. Create the document using a size other than 8.5-by-11-inch paper, or print the document with multiple pages as a poster.
3. Save the completed document with the name **8-Promotional**.
4. Print and then close **8-Promotional.docx**. (Attach the original document if one was used.)
5. Discuss the approach used to create this document with the rest of the class. Each member should participate in the presentation.

Figure WB-8.4 Sample Solution for Assessment 4

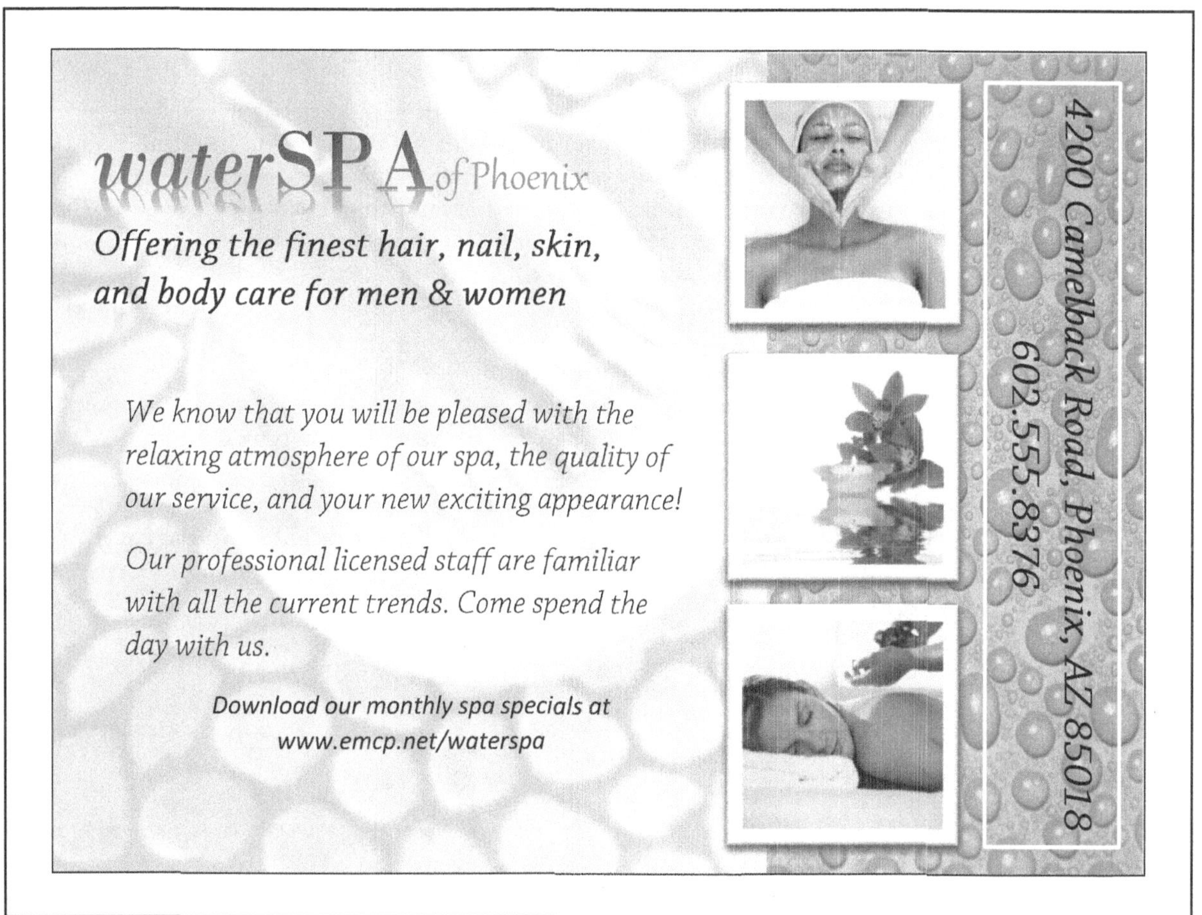

Visual Benchmark

Create an Integrated Application Form

Data Files

INTEGRATED

In this exercise, you will create a scholarship application form using a Word table. You will insert information from an Excel worksheet into the Word table. You will see that integrating Excel (with its automatic calculating features) into the Word form makes it easier to calculate totals. Create the scholarship application form with the following specifications:

1. At a blank document and using Figure WB-8.5 as a guide, create the scholarship application form shown in Figure WB-8.6. Insert a table and use the cells as placeholders for the information. Complete the form as shown in Figure WB-8.6 *except* do not insert the Community Services chart or the image in the row below the *Eligibility requirements* paragraph. ***Hint: Resize the column widths and row heights before merging the cells for the headings.***
2. Save the application form document that you created in Step 1 with the name **8-ScholarshipAppForm**. Leave the form open as you complete the following steps.
3. Open Excel and then open **CommunityServiceHours.xlsx**, in the C8 folder.
4. Add the AutoSum formula in cell B8 by positioning the insertion point in the cell, clicking the AutoSum button in the Editing group on the Home tab, typing B2:B7 in the formula, and then pressing the Enter key.
5. Select and then copy cells A1 through B8.
6. Click the Word button on the taskbar. (This should display **8-ScholarshipAppForm.docx** on the screen). Position the insertion point in the cell below the *Eligibility requirements* paragraph, click the Paste button arrow in the Clipboard group on the Home tab, and then click *Paste Special* at the drop-down list. At the Paste Special dialog box, click *Microsoft Excel Worksheet Object* in the *As* list box and then click OK.
7. Click the Excel button on the taskbar, close **CommunityServiceHours.xlsx**, and then close Excel.
8. Insert an image similar to the one shown in Figure WB-8.6.
9. Save **8-ScholarshipAppForm.docx**.
10. Save a copy of the document by clicking Save As and type the name **8-ScholarshipAppFormCompleted**.
11. Fill in the application form as shown in Figure WB-8.7. (Press the Tab key to move from one cell to the next.) To fill in the numbers in the Excel worksheet, double-click the worksheet and then type the numbers as shown in Figure WB-8.7. The total amount should automatically recalculate. Click outside the object to return to the Word editing functions.
12. Save, print, and then close **8-ScholarshipAppFormCompleted.docx**.

Figure WB-8.5 Using a Table to Create a Scholarship Form

1.2" cell width, align bottom right

1" cell width, align bottom right

1.1" cell width, align bottom right

1.4" cell width, align bottom left

1.2" cell width, align bottom left

1.1" cell width, align bottom left

table width 7", center table

0.5" row height

shading, White, Background 1, Darker 50%

SCHOLARSHIP APPLICATION FORM

Date:		SS#:		Gender:	
Last Name:		First Name:		Middle Initial:	
Street Address:					
City:		State:		ZIP:	
Email:		Home Phone:		Cell Phone:	

11-point Calibri

0.3" row height

16-point Calibri, bold

22-point Calibri, bold, White, Background 1, small caps

Major Area of Study

0.4" row height

0.2" row height

1" cell width

	Applied Science		Education
	Arts & Science		Fine Arts
	Business		Interdisciplinary Studies
			Other ____________

0.25" cell width

shading, Light Gray, Background 2, Darker 10%

High School Class Standing	**Intended Student Status**
Junior	Full-time (12 hours or more)
Senior	Half-time (9 to 11 hours)
Graduate	Half-time (6 to 8 hours)

0.5" cell width, align bottom center

Eligibility requiremen... 40 hours of ... out your four years of high school. Double-c... then fill in t... e volunteered in each category. The total h... tomatically...

1.75" cell width, align bottom left

0.5" cell width, align bottom center

12-pt Calibri, bold align center left

11-pt Calibri align top left

0.3" row height

0.7" row height

shading, Light Gray, Background 2, Darker 10%

Community Services

Day camp	
Fund-raising	
Government	
High school	
Homeless shelter	
Other	
Total	0

0.31" row height

11-pt Calibri align center

Thank you for your application. Please return to Kelly Cavanaugh, 22 Parrot Way, St. Paul, MN 55102.

Figure WB-8.6 Application Form for Visual Benchmark

SCHOLARSHIP APPLICATION FORM

Date: ________ SS#: ________ Gender: ________

Last Name: ________ First Name: ________ Middle Initial: ________

Street Address: ________________________

City: ________ State: ________ ZIP: ________

Email: ________ Home Phone: ________ Cell Phone: ________

Major Area of Study

_____ Applied Science
_____ Arts & Science
_____ Business
_____ Education
_____ Fine Arts
_____ Interdisciplinary Studies
_____ Other ________________

High School Class Standing

_____ Junior
_____ Senior
_____ Graduate

Intended Student Status

_____ Full-time (12 hours or more)
_____ Half-time (9 to 11 hours)
_____ Half-time (6 to 8 hours)

Eligibility requirements include a minimum of 40 hours of community service throughout your four years of high school. Double-click the chart below and then fill in the number of hours you have volunteered in each category. The total hours will be calculated automatically.

Community Services	
Day camp	
Fund-raising	
Government	
High school	
Homeless shelter	
Other	
Total	0

Thank you for your application. Please return to Kelly Cavanaugh, 22 Parrot Way, St. Paul, MN 55102.

Figure WB-8.7 Completed Application Form for Visual Benchmark

SCHOLARSHIP APPLICATION FORM

Date:	June 10, 2018	SS#:	000-55-5555	Gender:	Female
Last Name:	Gibson	First Name:	Allison	Middle Initial:	E.
Street Address:	231 Marietta Avenue East				
City:	Atlanta	State:	GA	ZIP:	30312
Email:	agibson@emcp.net	Home Phone:	404-555-3048	Cell Phone:	404-555-4122

Major Area of Study

____ Applied Science
____ Arts & Science
_x_ Business
____ Education
____ Fine Arts
____ Interdisciplinary Studies
____ Other ____________

High School Class Standing

____ Junior
_x_ Senior
____ Graduate

Intended Student Status

_x_ Full-time (12 hours or more)
____ Half-time (9 to 11 hours)
____ Half-time (6 to 8 hours)

Eligibility requirements include a minimum of 40 hours of community service throughout your four years of high school. Double-click the chart below and then fill in the number of hours you have volunteered in each category. The total hours will be calculated automatically.

Community Services	
Day camp	12
Fund-raising	22
Government	0
High school	15
Homeless shelter	6
Other	0
Total	55

Thank you for your application. Please return to Kelly Cavanaugh, 22 Parrot Way, St. Paul, MN 55102.

Case Study

Part 1

Data Files

As Paul Brewster's assistant at NorthWest Aviation, you have been given the task of preparing promotional documents. Use the company information and graphics that you have developed in previous Case Studies, as well as the information in the **NWAText.docx** document in the C8 folder. Create coasters (use the labels or table feature to include more than one coaster on a page) that include the company name, basic contact information, and logo. Use the Word 2016 elements you have learned in this book to enhance the design of the coasters and then save the document with the name **8-NWACoasters**. Print and then close **8-NWACoasters.docx**.

Part 2

Create NorthWest Aviation gift certificates for Mr. Brewster (use the labels or table feature to include more than one gift certificate on a page) that include the company name, basic contact information, and logo. Also include any labels and lines used to display data about the receiver of the certificate. Use the Word 2016 elements you have learned in this book to enhance the design of the gift certificates and then save the document with the name **8-NWACertificate**. Print and then close **8-NWACertificate.docx**.

Part 3

Data Files

Create NorthWest Aviation postcards, which will be mailed to potential and existing customers. Use one of Word's many features to include more than one postcard per page. Include the information about the discounted flight offer, which is provided in the **NWAText.docx** document. Also include the company name, address, and logo on the back side of the postcard. Use the Word 2016 elements you have learned in this book to enhance the design of the postcards and then save the document with the name **8-NWAPostCards**. Print and then close **8-NWAPostCards.docx**.

Part 4

Data Files

Design and print a NorthWest Aviation poster, which will be hung up around the local airports. Include the information about the discounted flight offer, which is provided in the **NWAText.docx** document. Also include the company name, basic contact information, and logo on the poster. Use the Word 2016 elements you have learned in this book to enhance the design of the poster and then save the document with the name **8-NWAPoster**. Use your printer's properties to print the poster on more than one page and then print **8-NWAPoster.docx**. Cut out the margin area on the pages and then assemble the poster.

Unit 2
Performance Assessment

Assessing Proficiency

In this unit, you have learned to apply design concepts to create flyers, newsletters, brochures, booklets, and other specialty promotional documents.

Data Files

Before beginning unit work, copy the U2 folder to your storage medium and then make U2 the active folder.

Assessment 1

Data Files

Prepare a Volunteer Newsletter

1. Open a document based on the template **SONewsletterTemplate.dotx** and then create a newsletter to be sent to the Summit Outreach volunteers (see Figure WB-U2.1 on page WB-87 for a sample solution) by completing the following steps (the template has already been formatted into two columns):
   a. For the text of the newsletter articles, insert text from the following documents from the U2 folder:
      DonationsNeeded.docx
      VolunteerOpportunities.docx
      DietaryChanges.docx
      HealthierChoices.docx
   b. Insert the Summit Outreach logo, **SOLogo.png**.
   c. Insert an appropriate image in at least one of the articles.
2. Save the document and name it **U2-SONewsletter**.
3. Print **U2-SONewsletter.docx**.
4. Save the document again in PDF format.
5. Close both documents.

Assessment 2

Create a Dental Services Flyer

You work for a dental clinic and are responsible for creating a flyer promoting clinic services. Using the table feature in Word, create the flyer shown in Figure WB-U2.2 on page WB-88 by completing the following steps:

1. At a blank document, change the top margin to 1.25 inches.
2. Insert a table with two columns and four rows and then make the following modifications to the table (refer to Figure WB-U2.2):
   a. Change the height of the first row to 1.7 inches, the second row to 3.9 inches, the third row to 1.1 inches, and the fourth row to 1.4 inches.
   b. Merge the cells in the first row and then use the Shading button in the Tables Styles group on the Table Tools Design tab to apply Blue, Accent 1, Darker 25% shading (fifth column, fifth row in the *Theme Colors* section) to the cell, as shown in Figure WB-U2.2.

c. Apply Blue, Accent 1, Darker 25% shading to the second cell in the second row and to the two cells in the bottom row.
d. Merge the two cells in the third row and then apply Blue, Accent 1, Lighter 40% shading (fifth column, fourth row in the *Theme Colors* section) to the cell, as shown in Figure WB-U2.2 on page WB-88.
e. Click in the first row and then change the alignment to Align Center. ***Hint: This button is located on the Table Tools Layout tab.***
f. Click in the third row and then change the alignment to Align Center Left.
g. Change the alignment of both cells in the fourth (bottom) row to Align Center Left.

3. Type the text shown in Figure WB-U2.2 in the cells and apply formatting by completing the following steps:
   a. Type Need a new smile? in the first row, change the font size to 56 points, and then use the Text Effects and Typography button to apply the Fill: White; Outline: Blue, Accent color 1; Glow: Blue, Accent color 1 text effect.
   b. Type the text in the second cell in the second column and then change the font size to 18 points and the font color to White, Background 1. ***Hint: You will need to press the Enter key before typing the text.***
   c. Type Call today! 800.555.1225 in the third row, change the font size to 36 points, and then use the Text Effects and Typography button to apply the Fill: White; Outline: Blue, Accent color 5; Shadow text effect.
   d. Type the text in the two cells in the bottom row, change the font size to 14 points, and change the font color to White, Background 1.
4. Insert **dentist.png** from the U2 folder, change the text wrapping to In Front of Text, and then position the image in the first cell in the second row as shown in Figure WB-U2.2.
5. Insert **tooth.png** from the U2 folder, change the height to 1.3 inches, change the text wrapping to In Front of Text, and then position the image in the third row as shown in Figure WB-U2.2.
6. Save the document with the name **U2-BriteSmileFlyer**.
7. Print and then close **U2-BriteSmileFlyer.docx**.

Figure WB-U2.1 Sample Solution for Assessment 1

Published for the Volunteers of Summit Outreach Community Services

Summit Outreach

Community Connections

Navigating Community Resources — Winter 2018

"We would be turning people away without food, which is totally unacceptable. Right now we're not even meeting people's food needs."

We need the following items:

- Personal care items such as shampoo, toothpaste, and deodorant
- Dishwashing liquid
- Laundry detergent, paper towels, and tissues

Our Vision
Navigating Community Resources

Our Mission
Summit Outreach provides resource referrals and leadership in the community by coordinating and uniting resources to empower people to be self-sufficient.

It's a bare time...

Nobody donates denture cleaners and adhesives, and there is never enough baby food to meet the outreach's monthly demand of 45 cases.

So, even in May when food donations are highest and the outreach's shelves are packed, Summit Outreach executive director Ryan Stratman must take a few trips to Target and Wal-Mart.

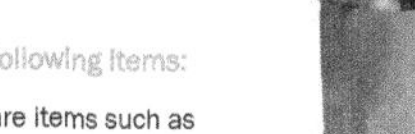

On average, the outreach spends $10,000 a month in an attempt to meet the food needs of needy area families. "When January and February roll around, food donations begin to decline. Nobody wants to go out in the cold and collect food," Stratman said.

Summit Outreach receives the bulk of its cash donations in November and December. The outreach would not survive without that money. "We would be turning people away without food, which is totally unacceptable," Stratman said. "Right now we are not even meeting people's food needs."

The outreach provides each family with three bags of groceries a month, and those groceries are valued at roughly $200. This time of the year, though, Summit Outreach has to buy most of that food. There are collections here and there.

"We would be turning pe... unacceptable. Right no...

Volunteer oppo...

Volunteers may register ... p.m. on Mondays, Tuesd... to 2 p.m. Groups are als... reserve a time.

The minimum age to wo... With a parent present, t... safety of all volunteers. ... consent form.

- Clean outreach ...
- Pick up grocerie...
- Assist with home...
- Work in the offic...
- Run errands
- Substitute for ba...
- Sort and shelve ...

Front

Summit Outreach
884 Alder Lane
Bellingham, WA 98225
Phone: (360) 555-8110
Fax: (360) 555-8115
summit@emcp.com
www.emcp.net/summit
As we are a registered 501(c)(3) charity, all donations are fully tax deductible.

Changes address dietary concerns

Summit Outreach strives to provide a variety of foods in accordance with the USDA Food Pyramid so clients can create balanced meals. Now, a new focus will be placed on meeting special dietary needs.

Executive Director Ryan Stratman said the change is part of ongoing efforts to continuously improve nutritional aspects of our food program. "We plan to address special needs our clients have indicated to us," he said. Among the most popular recent concerns were sugar-free and reduced sodium products. Lactose- and gluten-free products will also be stocked.

These foods are now available on a special cart near the three self-serve carts that currently contain mainly ethnic and cultural foods. Stratman said this would have to suffice for now. "Since our parking shortage prevents us from offering shopping opportunities, this is a key first step to meeting clients' special dietary needs and restrictions."

Reducing the amount of sodium in foods in all clients' bags is another goal. Since many of the healthier options also come in larger packaging, the shift would also increase the number of servings, an added bonus.

Part of this broad-reaching improvement is discontinuing the purchase of chili, canned pasta, and high sodium soup. Substitutions include healthy pasta sauce, doubling the canned tuna, providing extra cereal, and introducing shelf-stable, low-fat milk. Our goal is to limit sodium to less than 500 milligrams per serving, she added. The program is being implemented in two steps to provide clients with a smooth transition.

Healthier choices

Current Food	Healthier Option
2 Canned Pasta (4 servings) 810 mg sodium and 7 g of fat	1 Box Pasta (8 servings) 15 mg sodium and 3 g fat Spaghetti Sauce (5 servings) 255 mg sodium and .8 g fat
2 Canned Chili (4 servings) 800 mg sodium and 14 g fat	2 Canned Tuna (5 servings) 130 mg sodium and 0 g fat
4 Canned Soup (10 servings) 820 mg sodium and 5 g fat	1 Boxed Cereal (11 servings) 180 mg sodium and 1 g fat
1 Package American Cheese (16 servings) 290 mg sodium and 5 g fat	2 Shelf-Stable Milk (or cheese when milk is not available through NIFB) (8 servings) 110 mg sodium and 5 g fat
Total Servings: 36.5	**Total Servings: 40**

We're on the Web!
emcp.net/summit

Back

Figure WB-U2.2 Flyer Created in Assessment 2

Need a new smile?

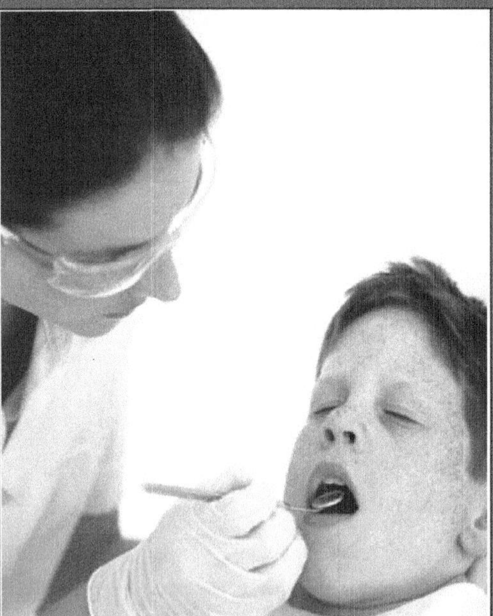

Come see us at Brite Smile!

- Veneers and implants
- Crowns and fillings
- Dentures
- Periodontal care
- Porcelain fillings
- Bonding
- Bridges
- Gentle care for children

Call today! 800.555.1225

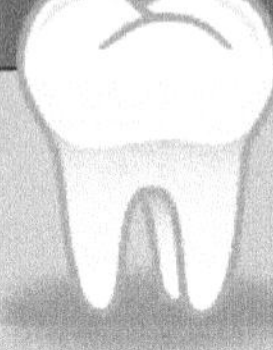

Brite Smile
Eastside Clinic
2194 East James Street
Jackson, MS 39026

Brite Smile
Westside Clinic
10338 West Tenth Avenue
Jackson, MS 39029

Assessment 3

Data Files

Create an Executive Search Fact Sheet

Using the text in **FactSheetText.docx**, create a fact sheet highlighting the services offered by Winston & McKenzie's Executive Search Services Department according to the following specifications (refer to Figure WB-U2.3 for a sample solution, but use your own design and formatting):

1. Experiment with the layout and design and then create a thumbnail sketch of what you propose for the fact sheet.
2. Insert **WMLogo.png** into the document.
3. Vary the use of fonts, type sizes, typestyles, and text effects to emphasize the relative importance of items.
4. Use bullets to create a list of the services offered. You choose the bullet style.
5. Include any relevant pictures, symbols, borders, colors, and so on in the fact sheet. Determine how to size and position the page elements and to apply shading, borders and fill, spacing, alignment, and so forth. ***Hint: Photographs tend to look more professional than clip art.***
6. Save the document with the name **U2-W&MFactSheet**.
7. Print and then close **U2-W&MFactSheet.docx**.
8. Open **DocumentEvaluationChecklist.docx** in the U2 folder and save the document with the name **U2-Analysis-3**. Use the checklist to evaluate your fact sheet.
9. Save, print, and then close **U2-Analysis-3.docx**. Hand in both the fact sheet and the evaluation checklist.

Figure WB-U2.3 Sample Solution for Assessment 3

Assessment

4

Data Files

Create a Self-mailing Facts Brochure

Using the text in **WMText1.docx**, **WMText2.docx**, and **WMText3.docx** in the U2 folder, create a self-mailing trifold brochure according to the following specifications (refer to Figure WB-U2.4 on page WB-92 for a sample solution, but use your own design and formatting). ***Reminder: Save periodically as you work through this assessment.***

1. Create a dummy of the brochure layout so you know exactly which panel will be used for each section of text.
2. Prepare a thumbnail sketch of your proposed layout and design.
3. At a blank document, set up the page by completing the following steps:
   a. Change the orientation to landscape.
   b. Change the top and bottom margins to 0.5 inch and the left and right margins to 0.45 inch.
   c. Change the gutter measurement to 0.25 inch.
4. Create the inside panels of the brochure according to the following specifications:
   a. Use columns, text boxes, or a table as the underlying structure for the brochure.
   b. Insert **WMText1.docx** in panel 1, **WMText2.docx** in panel 2, and **WMText3.docx** in panel 3.
   c. Choose appropriate typefaces, type sizes, and text effects to reflect the mood or tone of the brochure and the company it represents. ***Hint: If you are using columns, insert a column break to begin each new panel.***
   d. Consider using a drop cap, shape, watermark, or other design element to create focus.
   e. Apply bulleted formatting to the lists. You choose the bullet symbol, size, color, spacing, and so forth.
   f. Create new styles or modify existing styles to save time and keystrokes. You may want to create styles for the headings, body text, and bulleted items.
   g. Use text boxes to specifically position text or to highlight text in a unique way.
   h. Include ruled lines. Choose an appropriate line style, thickness, placement, and color.
5. To make the brochure a self-mailer, create the mailing address side of the request for information (created in panel 3) and insert the mailing information in panel 4 by completing the following steps:
   a. Insert the mailing address in a text box and then use the Text Direction button to rotate the mailing address 90 degrees. Choose an appropriate font, type size, and color. Type the following address:

      Winston & McKenzie, CPA
      Executive Search Services
      4600 North Meridian Street
      Indianapolis, IN 46240

   b. Size and position the text box containing the mailing address in an appropriate position.
   c. Leave panel 5 blank because it will be the back side of the self-mailer. Once a person fills out the information in panel 3, he or she will refold the brochure so that panel 4, the self-mailer panel, will be on top.

6. Create the cover of the brochure in panel 6 by completing the following steps:
   a. Type You Can't Afford to Make the Wrong Hiring Decision! as the title of the brochure.
   b. Insert **WMLogo.png** from the U2 folder and then size and position the logo.
   c. Choose an appropriate location for the company name and address and for the following phone and fax numbers, and then type the information in that location:

      Phone: (317) 555-8900
      Fax: (317) 555-6901
      Email: winmck@emcp.net
      Web: emcp.net/winmck
7. Save the brochure with the name **U2-Brochure**.
8. Print and then close **U2-Brochure.docx**.
9. Open **DocumentEvaluationChecklist.docx** from the U2 folder and then save the document with the name **U2-Analysis-4**. Use the checklist to evaluate your brochure. Make any changes that are necessary.
10. Save, print, and then close **U2-Analysis-4.docx**. Hand in both the brochure and the evaluation checklist.

Assessment 5

Create a Fashion Show Invitation

Use the table feature to create an invitation for a fashion show according to the following specifications:

1. Use Word's table feature to create the cover of an invitation in landscape orientation. If you can find an appropriate template, feel free to use and customize it.
2. Type the following information on the cover of the invitation: Act II Theater's Fifth Annual Fashion Show. Add graphics, watermarks, lines, borders, symbols, and other enhancements to the invitation cover (see Figure WB-U2.5A on page WB-93 for a sample solution).
3. Save the completed cover with the name **U2-InvitationCover**.
4. Print and then close **U2-InvitationCover.docx**.
5. Use the table feature to create the inside of the invitation. Using Figure WB-U2.5B as a reference, type the following information on the inside of the invitation:

   Please join us for the fifth annual Fashion Show fund-raising event for Act II Theater, Friday, May 11.
   Benaroya Hall, 300 Connor Street
   Social hour: 6:30 to 7:30 p.m.
   Fashion show: 7:30 to 8:30 p.m.
   All proceeds fund the youth community theater project.
6. Add graphics, watermarks, lines, borders, symbols, and other enhancements to the inside of the invitation (see Figure WB-U2.5B for a sample solution).
7. Save the completed invitation with the name **U2-InvitationInside**.
8. Print and then close **U2-InvitationInside.docx**.

Figure WB-U2.4 Sample Solution for Assessment 4

Identifying, Assessing, and Hiring Senior Officers

Your executive management team is critical to your institution's success. However, selecting the right individuals is not easy. Hiring the wrong candidates can cost your institution as much as two times their salary in wasted recruiting and training expenses, lost productivity, and lowered morale.

Winston & McKenzie, CPA, can help you make more effective staffing decisions. We do more than simply take job specs over the phone and send you a stack of résumés. We work with you to initially evaluate the position to determine whether it should be filled, altered, or eliminated. Once the decision to fill a position is made, we can conduct the entire search, parts of the process, or simply coach you through the process. Your needs determine our level of involvement.

Our search consultants utilize Winston & McKenzie's full range of specialized financial institution resources to enhance your search.

You Select the Services that Meet Your Needs

- ✓ Defining the position
- ✓ Handling internal candidates
- ✓ Generating candidates
- ✓ Assessing candidates
- ✓ Conducting interviews
- ✓ Testing candidates
- ✓ Performing reference and background checks
- ✓ Assisting with employment offers

I Would Like More Information...

on how Winston & McKenzie can help my institution find and hire the right management team.

For more information about our Executive Search Services please call:

Janet Rankins at (317) 555-6342
Email: winmck@emcp.net

Visit our website at:

emcp.net/winmck

or complete the information request card below.

Name: ____________________
Institution: ____________________
Address: ____________________
City: ____________________
State: ____________________
ZIP: ____________________
Email: ____________________
Telephone: ____________________
Cell: ____________________

Winston & McKenzie, CPA
Executive Search Services
4600 North Meridian Street
Indianapolis, IN 46240

You Can't Afford to Make the Wrong Hiring Decision!

Winston & McKenzie, CPA
Executive Search Services
4600 North Meridian Street
Indianapolis, IN 46208

Phone: (317) 555-8900
Fax: (317) 555-6901
Email: winmck@emcp.net
Web: emcp.net/winmck

Figure WB-U2.5 Sample Solution for Assessment 5

A
Cover of Invitation

B
Inside of Invitation

DTP Challenge

Take your skills to the next level by completing this more challenging assessment.

Assessment

6

Create a Virtual Office Resource Guide

1. Create a resource guide for a virtual office. Conduct research about resources you think would be valuable to someone operating a business from home, such as helpful websites, commercial printers, computer repair companies, office supply companies, airports, limousine and taxi companies, local conference centers (hotels with conference room availability), restaurants for business meetings, community clubs and organizations for entrepreneurs, community college virtual office courses, and temporary office employment companies.
2. Format the resource information in booklet format. ***Hint: Use the 2 Pages per Sheet or book fold feature to format the booklet.***
3. Allow enough space to add additional resources to the document in the future.
4. Use appropriate graphics, fonts, tables, footers, and so on.
5. Use styles to reinforce consistency in the design.
6. Save the document with the name **U2-VirtualResourceGuide**.
7. Print and then close **U2-VirtualResourceGuide.docx**.